AVY JOSEPH + MAGGIE CHAPMAN

CONFIDENCE

&

SUCCESS

WITH

CBT

SMALL STEPS TO ACHIEVE YOUR BIG GOALS WITH COGNITIVE BEHAVIOUR THERAPY

CAPSTONE
A Wiley Brand

Cover design by Parent Design Ltd

© 2013 Avy Joseph and Maggie Chapman

Registered office

Capstone Publishing Ltd. (A Wiley Company), John Wiley and Sons, Ltd., The Atrium, Southern Gate, Chichester, West Sussex, PO19 8SQ, United Kingdom

For details of our global editorial offices, for customer services and for information about how to apply for permission to reuse the copyright material in this book please visit our website at www.wiley.com.

Library of Congress Cataloging-in-Publication Data

Joseph, Avy.

  Confidence and success with CBT : small steps to achieve your big goals with cognitive behaviour therapy / Avy Joseph and Maggie Chapman.

      1 online resource.

  Includes index.

  Description based on print version record and CIP data provided by publisher; resource not viewed.

  ISBN 978-0-85708-347-0 (ebk) – ISBN 978-0-85708-348-7 (ebk) – ISBN 978-0-85708-349-4 (ebk) – ISBN 978-0-85708-350-0 (pbk.)   1. Cognitive therapy.   2. Psychotherapy–Methodology.   I. Chapman, Maggie, 1954–   II. Title.

  RC489.C63

  616.89'1425–dc23

  2013022091

A catalogue record for this book is available from the British Library.

ISBN 978-0-857-08350-0 (pbk)   ISBN 978-0-857-08348-7 (ebk)
ISBN 978-0-857-08349-4 (ebk)   ISBN 978-0-857-08347-0 (ebk)

Set in 10/13.5 pt Adobe Caslon Pro-Regular by Toppan Best-set Premedia Limited
Printed in Great Britain by TJ International Ltd, Padstow, Cornwall, UK

CONFIDENCE
&
SUCCESS
WITH
CBT

To our families, friends and colleagues, who support us so brilliantly.

Contents

Confidence and Success

"We are what we think; all that we are arises with our thoughts; with our thoughts we make our world."

Buddha

Confidence gives you the power to be able to fully focus on your goals without being anxious. This means you do not dwell on potential negative consequences but remain focused on the task at hand. You are not anxious about failure or the disapproval of others, and nor are you disturbed when you fail.

The mindset that creates confidence increases the probability of enjoyment and success. Belief in your ability to achieve a task is influenced by successful experiences that reinforce a more general sense of self-confidence. When we feel confident, we focus on achieving what we set out to do, in the present moment and in a constructive way. If we lack confidence, we may hear ourselves say, "If only I could feel more confident", "I can't do this" or "I'm not good enough", "I have never succeeded at anything", "I don't think I can do it", "I don't know how I did this" or "That was a fluke."

Confidence arises from experience and a healthy mindset. A good example of this is when we learn to drive a car. Initially, we have little confidence in our ability, and rightly so, but as we learn and practise the new skills we become more confident in our ability to perform them. We feel uncomfortable when we start learning how to drive but with determination, a focus on the goal and repeated practice we develop a growing sense of confidence in our ability to drive.

Success is felt when we achieve the goals we set for ourselves. Success is a personal experience and it depends on what each of us wants. It is the conscious awareness that we are doing what we want to do in a self-determined way that denotes success. For some, success may be:

- A garden that produces enough not to require a visit to the supermarket.
- Living life fully enjoying each day with a sense of contentment and well-being.
- Buying a house/car.
- Being in a healthy relationship.
- £x millions in the bank account.
- An Olympic gold medal.
- Reaching a target weight.
- Securing a promotion at work.

Developing confidence and success involves identifying what you want and setting about achieving it while overcoming the obstacles as and when they occur. We have identified six key steps to help you realise your goal, whatever it may be. They are:

- Step 1: Identify what you want.
- Step 2: Gather information.
- Step 3: Set achievable goals.
- Step 4: Create a plan.
- Step 5: Take action.
- Step 6: Keep focus on the goal with feedback.

We have seen, over the years, in both our corporate and private practices many individuals who struggle with self-confidence, failure and a perception of failure, as well as a host of other issues. At the heart of the problem with confidence and success is anxiety. Anxieties can be about discomfort, failure, disapproval, uncertainty, perfectionism and so forth. Confidence and success are sabotaged by holding unhealthy beliefs.

The aim of this book is to use the cognitive behaviour therapy (CBT) model to help you understand:

- The mindset required to achieve your bigger goal.
- The mindset that creates obstacles to success.
- How to overcome the obstacles by changing your beliefs.
- How to develop confidence.

First though, it is necessary to explain in more detail the basic principles of CBT and the central role that beliefs play in this model.

"It is not enough to take steps which may some day lead to a goal; each step must be itself a goal and a step likewise."

Johann Wolfgang von Goethe

Using CBT

CBT Theory

"It is not the event but the view we take of it that disturbs us."
Epictetus

Epictetus eloquently sums up Cognitive Behaviour Therapy (CBT). CBT looks at how we think and what we do. It takes the view that emotions, like anxiety, arise from faulty thinking. That is to say, essentially, we are largely responsible for our emotions, thoughts and behaviours.

We tend to speak in a way that suggests events, people, situations or objects can make us feel or do things. Someone could say, "Presentations make me panic." This is clearly not the case. If this were true, everyone who did a presentation would panic. There has to be something else that provokes panic. It is called a "belief". Therefore, it is the belief about presentations that provokes those feelings of panic and not the presentations themselves.

In the following steps, we are going to look at specific types of unhealthy beliefs that provoke unhealthy feelings, thoughts and behaviours. For example, a belief such as "I must succeed at all costs because failure would be like the end of the world for me" would provoke emotional disturbance, such as anxiety, and may lead to avoidant behaviour.

Consider the following illustration to understand this concept.

The Simple ABC Model

This simple model illustrates the basic theoretical principles of CBT and the effect our beliefs have on our feelings and behaviours. It also illustrates the principles of emotional responsibility. It reminds us that it is not the event but the belief or view we hold about the event that provokes our feelings and behaviours.

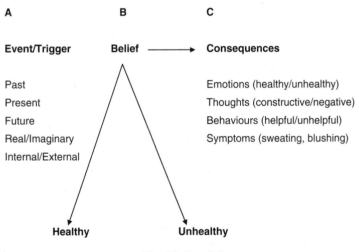

A	B	C
Event/Trigger	Belief ⟶	Consequences
Past		Emotions (healthy/unhealthy)
Present		Thoughts (constructive/negative)
Future		Behaviours (helpful/unhelpful)
Real/Imaginary		Symptoms (sweating, blushing)
Internal/External		
Healthy		Unhealthy

The ABC model

- The event at A can be something that has happened in the past or it may be happening now, or it could be something that might happen in the future. A can also be real or imagined and internal (in the form of memories or images, physical sensations or emotions) or it can be an external event.

- The B is the healthy or unhealthy belief you hold about the event at A.
- The C is the consequential responses that are provoked by the belief at B. These can take the form of emotions, thoughts, behaviours or physical symptoms.

A particular CBT psychotherapeutic model known as REBT (Rational Emotive Behaviour Therapy) teaches us to recognise unhealthy thinking and develop new beliefs and attitudes that lead to confidence and success. Ellis (see box) believed that we have little choice about being human so it is preferable not to put ourselves down but to remember that we have choices and alternatives. We can develop healthy beliefs to aid us in the pursuit of our goals. We can experiment, experience, learn and change what doesn't work. We can develop resilience rather than anxiety about disappointment and failures.

REBT is both evidence-based and philosophical. The theory was developed by psychologist Albert Ellis, PhD, who first articulated the principles of REBT in 1955. Albert Ellis was born in 1913 in Pittsburgh, Pennsylvania, but moved to New York at age four. He was hospitalised numerous times during childhood, and suffered renal glycosuria at age 19 and diabetes at age 40. Because Ellis suffered from these ailments for most of his life, his problems inspired him over the years to find effective means of coping.

Understanding Unhealthy and Healthy Beliefs

We tend to transform desires, wants and preferences into rigid, dogmatic and absolute beliefs. The word "belief" means a conviction in the truth or validity of something. When beliefs are unrealistic, non-sensical and unhelpful to us, they are irrational or unhealthy. Such beliefs are at the heart of our problems with confidence.

Unhealthy Beliefs

Unhealthy or irrational beliefs are rigid, nonsensical, inconsistent with reality and unhelpful in the pursuit of your goals. Healthy or rational beliefs are flexible, make sense, are consistent with reality and helpful in the pursuit of your goals.

Unhealthy beliefs are based on absolutist shoulds, musts, have tos and need tos (e.g. "I absolutely should be able to do this"). This is not the kind of should as in "I should go shopping" but rather an absolutist should with a capital "S", a demand.

Flowing from these demands are three irrational derivative beliefs:

- **Awfulising** – a belief about an irrational assessment of badness. It views the bad event not just as bad but as 100% bad (i.e. end-of-the-world bad; nothing else is worse in that moment). It is often expressed as: "It is a disaster", "It is horrible/awful/terrible", "It is a catastrophe" or "It is the end of the world."
- **Low frustration tolerance (LFT)** – a belief that underestimates your ability to cope with an adverse event and is often expressed as: "It is intolerable", "I can't cope", "I can't stand it" or "It is too hard."
- **Self-damning** – a belief where you judge yourself in a globally dismissive, totally negative way. It is expressed as: "I am a loser", "I am a failure", "I am weak", "I am stupid", "I am worthless", "I am useless" or "I am an idiot."

Healthy Beliefs

Alternatively, healthy beliefs are based on preferences, wants, wishes and desires without the dogmatic demand. They help us remain focused on what we want with an acceptance of the possibility that it may not happen. Accepting that something may not go our way does not mean we like or approve of it. Acceptance means that we are not disturbed by disappointments and failures.

Flowing from these preferences are three rational derivative beliefs, the helpful alternatives to the irrational derivative beliefs we discussed earlier:

- **Anti-awfulising** – a belief that views negative events as bad with the badness placed on a continuum of 0–99.9% bad, where 100% bad does not exist, as one can usually think of something worse, e.g. "It would be bad but not the end of the world if I didn't achieve my goal."
- **High frustration tolerance (HFT)** – a belief that does not underestimate your ability to tolerate frustration or discomfort despite having your goals blocked, e.g. "It would be very difficult not to achieve my goal but I can tolerate it: it won't kill me."
- **Self-acceptance** – a belief that you are a worthwhile but fallible human being regardless of anyone or anything. It is based on unconditional self-acceptance, where you judge your performance, behaviour or success but not your worth, e.g. "I don't like the fact that I failed but that does not make me a failure as a human being. I remain worthwhile but fallible."

Wanting to achieve and succeed, to receive approval and comfort, is true for most of us. But liking or wanting something does not make it a universal law of Nature that we must have it. If it were, all of us would always achieve, always succeed, always have approval and always have comfort. This is not what we see in real life. Healthy beliefs enable us to focus on our goals in a positive way by freeing us from anxiety, because we recognise that the end of the world is not nigh, that we are able to tolerate difficulties and that we are worthwhile and fallible despite failures and disappointments. This is the attitude that builds confidence and increases the likelihood of success.

Emotions, Thoughts, Behaviours and Physical Symptoms

You will notice from the ABC diagram that beliefs provoke consequences. These are emotions, thoughts, behaviours and physical symptoms. Since beliefs can be healthy or unhealthy, so too can their consequences.

Emotions

REBT identifies eight unhealthy negative emotions and eight healthy counterparts.

- Unhealthy negative emotions are: anxiety, depression, anger/rage, hurt, shame/embarrassment, guilt, unhealthy envy and jealousy.
- Healthy negative emotions are: concern, sadness, annoyance, disappointment, remorse, regret, healthy envy and concern for one's relationships.

Thoughts

Unhealthy beliefs provoke unhelpful thoughts and assumptions. The mind is preoccupied with "what ifs" rather than focusing on the task at hand. For example, in a state of anxiety, you would overestimate the negative consequences of a future threat or risk and underestimate your ability to cope. Healthy beliefs provoke more realistic thoughts and assumptions that are constructive and solution-focused. For example, you would be realistic in your assessment of risk and your ability to cope.

Behaviours

Unhealthy beliefs provoke a tendency to behave in an unhelpful manner.

Behaviour is usually an expression of these tendencies. People usually, but not always, act in accordance with what they feel like doing. In a state of anxiety, it is common for people to feel like withdrawing from the task in hand, and in most cases they will also act in accordance with those feelings (i.e. avoid). Healthy beliefs tend to provoke constructive action tendencies and behaviours. This means you will take action to achieve your goal.

Physical Symptoms

Unhealthy beliefs provoke physical symptoms such as blushing, sweating, irritable bowel syndrome, physical tension and many other symptoms.

Healthy beliefs also provoke physical symptoms, such as discomfort and tension. This happens because even though healthy beliefs are based on what we want there is an acceptance of the negative possibility of not succeeding. The tension is a response to this potentially negative event.

These can be intense, but if the belief is healthy, the mindset will still be constructive and solution-focused – despite the tension in the body.

It is important to realise that tension in itself is not an indication that there is something wrong. If the mindset is negative then the tension felt is provoked by the unhealthy belief. If the mindset is constructive then the tension is provoked by the healthy belief. By having a healthy mindset and a focus on the goal, tension is more easily tolerated.

Three Major Themes of Disturbance

Albert Ellis noted that we tend to disturb ourselves about three major themes:

- The demand to perform well or outstandingly at all times.
- The demand for others to treat us nicely, considerately or fairly at all times.
- The demand for life to be comfortable and hassle-free.

When these demands are not met, we tend to disturb ourselves. This means we feel stuck, anxious, depressed and act in self-defeating ways. Throughout this book, we will refer to these three major themes that give rise to the specific obstacles in each step. The purpose of doing this is to help you remember that essentially all of your specific unhealthy beliefs stem from these three roots.

How to Use This Book

Now that you have had an overview of CBT, it is helpful for you to understand how to use this book to get the most out of it. CBT is about changing unhealthy beliefs to healthy ones. To do this takes time, just as it takes time to learn a skill (like driving). It requires the repeated practice of new healthy beliefs stated with conviction, often while still experiencing negative emotions and discomfort until, as with all learning, it begins to feel more comfortable. The emotional change happens last and requires changes in behaviour as you determinedly apply the new healthy beliefs. Understanding alone will not create a change.

The steps that follow will take you through the six consecutive stages to identify and attain your goal, to achieve the success and confidence you desire. Each step is one small step towards your overall goal. Achieving each step is a smaller goal in its own right. With the achievement of each step, your confidence will most probably increase.

In each step, we have identified common obstacles in the form of unhealthy beliefs that sabotage the achievement of that step. There may be other obstacles that we have not discussed, of course, so there is an exercise at the end of each chapter that will help you identify any unhealthy beliefs and how to challenge them. You may find that some chapters are more relevant to your experience. For example, if you know how to set goals, maybe moving on to one of the later chapters will be more helpful to you.

Three arguments are deliberately repeated throughout the book to help you develop the habit of thinking in a helpful and progressive manner:

Reality check: Is there any evidence to say it is true?

Common sense: Is it logical to state this?

Helpfulness: No amount of unhelpful thinking will bring a solution.

The way in which we change our beliefs is through repetition, in a consistent and forceful manner. Identifying your unhealthy beliefs and challenging them with these three main arguments is a key strategy in changing them. It initially feels awkward but with repetition and consistency will, eventually, become a habit and feel effortless. You will learn that the solution to changing your unhealthy belief lies in adopting a healthy belief and behaving in accordance with that healthy belief.

The last chapter will then look at what you do once you have achieved your goal and how to move forward.

The case studies we have used are fictional but informed by actual cases. We have chosen quotes to inspire and sometimes to remind you that whatever difficulties you may be experiencing others have encountered the same issues. Finally, at the end of each chapter, there are some tips to summarise what has been said, just in case you forget!

> "In order to succeed, your desire for success should be greater than your fear of failure."
>
> *Bill Cosby*

Step 1

Identify What You Want

"To accomplish great things, we must not only act, but also dream; not only plan, but also believe."
Anatole France

Success is about achieving your goals, so naturally the first step towards your ultimate goal is identifying what you want. If you already know what you want then you can move to Step 2 in the next chapter; otherwise, this step is about reflecting and exploring what you want to achieve and work towards. It's important to keep in mind that this is not a time to think about what is possible or not. This step is about employing your imagination to guide you to your goal, as the initial step. You are just thinking: you are not taking action at the moment.

You may have never asked yourself the question "What do I want?" You may find yourself thinking, "I don't know. I've never really thought about it." If you want to experience a more fulfilling life, it is helpful to think about what you want from it. Human beings are naturally goal-seeking, and thinking about what we want can bring some benefits, such as:

- You may experience a sense of control and determination over your life as you consider new possibilities.
- Your mind will be occupied with the question "What do I want to achieve?" This invokes a natural problem-solving ability.
- You may experience a sense of anticipation and excitement as you begin thinking about what you want and the changes you may want to make.

The problem for many of us is not knowing what we really want. This question can only be answered through a period of self-reflection. It is not important that we answer our questions perfectly, but it is important to attempt to answer them and to clarify them. To help consider what is worthwhile and of value to you, look at the life wheel diagram. It gives examples of some areas in life that may be significant to you. It is only a guide and you may wish to add or remove something on the wheel. For example, replace "career" with "retirement" or add "sporting achievement" or "travel".

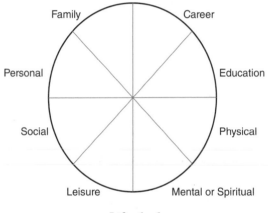

Life wheel

Start by choosing an area in your life that you might like to focus on and begin reflecting and writing a description of what it is you would like to achieve in that, and/or any other, area which interests you. There are no right or wrong choices as much will depend on where you are in your life currently: your age and personal circumstances etc. This stage is very much about exploring in a general way. As you move to the later steps, you can make what you want more focused and specific.

As you consider the different areas in your life, it is helpful to ask yourself some questions to help provoke your thought processes. Here are some general questions that may get you thinking.

- What do you enjoy?
- What do you dislike?
- What are your innate skills?
- What are your strengths?
- What are your weaknesses?
- What are the possibilities?
- Which of those possibilities are the most mouth-watering?
- Which do you like most?

Sometimes, it can also be helpful to consider the things you definitely know you do not want in your life before you consider what you do want.

As you begin to decide what area of your life you wish to focus on, you can begin to make your questions more specific to that area. For example, if you want to focus on your career, you could ask yourself some of the following questions.

- Am I happy with my current career?
- What career would I like to pursue?
- Is further training helpful?
- Is retraining a good idea?
- Do I want to travel in my job?
- Do I want to work abroad?
- What do I really like doing?

Example 1: Identify what you want – Working with animals

Let's say you love animals but are working in a completely unrelated field and are dissatisfied with that part of your life and so want to make a change. You begin to think that you would love to work with animals. You may have a particular animal you prefer. And so you begin to allow yourself to imagine just what your dream occupation and life would be like if you were working with animals.

You may want to ask yourself some more questions:

- Would it be as an animal activist or in animal rescue, or what?
- Where would I like to do this?
- Would it be in my home town or in a remote part of the world?
- Alone or with other people?
- Do I want to work for someone else or for myself?
- What would being successful actually look like?
- How much would I earn?

Keep reflecting and exploring and begin to rule out what you don't want to do until you have identified what you really do want to do.

It is important to remember to apply yourself to this step and take time on a regular basis to think about the question. It is often very helpful to write down the questions and answers when you find them. You can also keep a list of ideas, adding to it as more come into your mind. Taking action – in this instance by writing questions, answers and ideas down – demonstrates a commitment to your desire for change. There is no recommended time to take on this step. The key to success at this stage is to identify what you want, feel excited or passionate about it. Do not set yourself a time limit. This step is creating a vision or aspiration; the steps that follow will guide you to achieving it. For the moment, do not spend time thinking about *how* this is going to happen. This is the time for *what* questions. You will begin to know when you are on the right track when you begin to get that sense of anticipation about a particular idea.

Once you have identified what it is you want and desire in your life, you can begin to make it happen by gathering information. When you begin to take action, you begin to experience success, which leads to increased feelings of confidence, which in turn leads to more success.

Case study: Joanna – Discovering what I want

Joanna is struggling with her office job. She is unhappy with her office relationships and beginning to doubt herself and her abilities. She has started to experience increasing anxiety. Joanna came to therapy for help with her anxiety. Like so many people, she is doing a job she does not enjoy and so is not really performing to her abilities. Her feelings of anxiety and depression, owing to work, are affecting her life outside of work.

Joanna isn't sure what she wants to do with her life. She has small children, needs to contribute to the family income and feels "stuck". When Joanna is asked what she would really like to do, she replies that she has always wanted to run her own fitness gym. She can remember being a little girl and thinking that that was what she wanted when she grew up. She had even imagined just what it would be like. She laughs and says she knows that it would never really be possible and that it is just a dream, that it could never happen, that she would never be able to do it.

Solution

By recalling and talking about her childhood dream, she recognises she would still love to own and run her own gym. She allows herself the possibility that maybe her dream could be turned into reality.

By following the steps in this book, Joanna now runs a successful group of small gyms and has done so for the last eight years. She continues to expand her business.

Obstacles to Step 1: Identify What You Want

This first step can often be the hardest. It is the start of the change process. Thinking about future goals can trigger some obstacles to achieving this step.

The following are two common obstacles that provoke anxiety and avoidance:

1. I don't know what I want, even after reflecting and exploring.
2. Thinking about what I want is too much effort.

Unhealthy beliefs are at the root of these obstacles. Earlier, we talked about unhealthy beliefs and their healthy counterparts and how beliefs affect how we think, feel and behave. The next section will look at both of these obstacles separately and identify the types of unhealthy beliefs that underpin them.

Obstacle 1: "I don't know what I want, even after reflecting and exploring" and how to overcome it

Anxiety about not knowing what you want although you have reflected and explored can stop you even starting this step. The unhealthy belief will take the form of the general following theme.

I must achieve what I have set out to do.

The above attitude will give rise to many offshoot beliefs and specific beliefs, such as:

- I must know what I want to do after I have reflected and explored and if I don't I couldn't bear not knowing.
- I must know what I want to do after I have reflected and explored and if I don't it would be awful.
- I must know what I want to do after reflecting and exploring and if I don't know what I want after I have explored possibilities it means I am stupid and worthless.

When you demand that you must know what you want even after reflecting and exploring, you will tend to stop yourself beginning the process. Demanding that you must know at the end of this step does not allow for the possibility of not knowing. Holding this belief will disturb you, as it provokes feelings of anxiety. Accepting the possibility that you may not know what you want after spending time considering it will enable you to start and to continue to search for what you do want.

Reality Check

Gravity is a universally accepted law. It applies to everyone. Just jump up: you will eventually fall back down. There is no such law, however, which states that everyone must know what they want after reflecting upon it. If there were, it would mean that everyone would, after a first attempt of reflecting, know what they wanted to do. Of course, many of us will have worked out what we want from life after reflecting on it. But not everyone. Yet all is not lost for those people. After all, not accepting there is a chance you may still not know what you want after reflection doesn't alter the reality that it's still a possibility.

Common Sense

It is perfectly reasonable to want to know what you want to do after reflecting. However, it does not necessarily mean that you must know what you want afterwards. Most of us would certainly start a task with a desire for a positive outcome. However, it doesn't make sense to insist that we absolutely must achieve a positive outcome. Demanding that you must know what you want after reflecting about it does not make sense. Accepting that you may not know what you want after reflecting will enable you to continue your search.

Helpfulness

Holding the belief that you must know what you want to do after reflecting is unhelpful. It would provoke anxiety at the thought of starting to consider what you want. You would begin to have all sorts of thoughts provoked by this belief to persuade yourself not to start looking. Demanding you must know what you want to do after reflecting will sabotage your desire to achieve any goals before you even begin.

9

Low Frustration Tolerance (LFT)

LFT is a belief that underestimates your ability to cope with an adverse event and is often expressed as: "It is intolerable", "I can't cope", "I can't stand it" or "It is too hard."

LFT is linked to a demand, for example: "I must know what I want after reflecting and exploring and if not I couldn't bear not knowing." LFT is about effort, difficulty, frustration and anyone who's triggered into thinking that they cannot stand, tolerate or bear something will have LFT.

Reality Check

There is no truth in the belief that you cannot bear not knowing what you want to do after reflecting and exploring. You will not break if you do not know what you want to do after attempting to discover it. You are able to bear the discomfort of not knowing even though it may not be enjoyable. You will not fall apart.

Common Sense

It is nonsensical to believe that because you do not know what you want, even after exploring the possibilities, you cannot bear the fact that you don't. It would be true that you would experience discomfort and frustration, but it is also true that you would still be alive, bearing it. In life sometimes it takes many attempts to find what we want to do, and this unhealthy belief will stop any further exploration because it underestimates your resilience to handle the frustration.

 **Helpfulness**

Believing you would not bear it if you did not know what you wanted to do after your reflection is unhelpful. The LFT belief is unhelpful to you: it will not only prevent you from further exploration but also provoke anxiety and avoidant behaviours, making clear identification of your goal far less likely.

Awfulising

Awfulising is an unhealthy/irrational belief that when a demand is not fulfilled the badness is viewed as 100% or more bad (i.e. end-of-the-world bad, nothing else is worse in that moment). It is often expressed as: "It is a disaster", "It is awful/terrible/horrible", "It is a catastrophe" or "It is the end of the world."

When we hold an awfulising belief such as "I must know what I want to do after reflecting and exploring and if I don't it would be awful", we can experience feelings of anxiety or a sense of hopelessness, which in extreme forms can lead to depression.

 **Reality Check**

The unhealthy belief that it would be awful if you still didn't know what you wanted to do after you have finished your reflection is not true. There are many things that are worse. Many of us do not know what we want to do yet and the world still revolves around the sun. We can definitely prove that. And you will still continue to get up, clean your teeth, eat your food and so on: the world will not have ended.

Common Sense

It doesn't make sense to believe that it is awful if you still don't know what you want to do, after you have completed your reflection. It would be true that you may view that as bad or even very bad, but just because it is bad it doesn't follow that it is awful. Viewing something as awful is a nonsensical view to take about badness.

Helpfulness

The third challenge to the awfulising belief is whether it is helpful for you to hold this belief. Holding this belief that it is awful is unhelpful in your discovery of knowing what it is you do want to do. Viewing it as awful mobilises your body into a state of anxiety. In this state, your mind will be preoccupied with questions such as, "What if I have doubts?" and "What if I still don't know?" It prompts avoidance. The most likely outcome will be you not achieving this first simple step that takes you closer to your goal.

Self-damning

Self-damning is an unhealthy/irrational and wholly negative judgement of oneself based on the non-fulfilment of a demand. Often expressed as, "I'm worthless", "I'm not good enough", "I'm a failure" or "I'm stupid" and so on.

Some people will put themselves down if their demands are not met. It means that they only accept themselves if some condition is fulfilled. One of the key factors in self-acceptance is the recognition that we, as human beings, are all worthwhile and may judge or evaluate our behaviours but not the entire self. The fact that you may fail at something, in this case achieving "knowing", does not make you less worthy as a human being. It can be a central factor governing whether you are confident in yourself. When you damn yourself as stupid, weak or worthless, you are globally rating yourself, in essence believing that nothing positive exists about you in that moment.

Reality Check

Believing that you are "stupid and worthless" if you didn't manage to figure out what you want to do, even after taking time to reflect, is absurd. This generalisation about yourself ignores all your qualities, strengths and abilities. This belief is rigid and dogmatic and does not allow room for change: you have globally rated yourself negatively even though there will be evidence to oppose this belief. We all have strengths and weaknesses. All humans are fallible and fail as well as succeed. It is wrong to rate your worth on not knowing one particular thing in one particular instance: it ignores the many times when you do know the answer.

Common Sense

It makes no sense to globally rate yourself in this dogmatic fashion. When you hold a self-damning belief about not knowing something, it doesn't make sense to leap into believing "I'm therefore stupid and worthless". The truth of the matter is that you failed to figure out what you want, even after reflecting. That's it, no further leaps are required. To damn yourself for not being able to know what you want even after you have spent time exploring does not makes sense.

☺ Helpfulness

Holding the belief "I am stupid and worthless" because you have not found out what it is that you want to do is a self-limiting and unhelpful belief that does not assist you in finding what it is you do want to do. If you hold this self-damning belief you will prevent yourself, in all likelihood, from making any further attempts to find out what you want. All you do is crush your confidence in yourself. Does this, in any way, help you move closer to your goal?

Case study: Jack – Not knowing what I want

Jack chose a degree without a clear idea of what he wanted to do in his life and having received no particular guidance as to which direction to take. After graduation, he took a personality test, which suggested counselling as a career, but instead he went on to take a graduate job in sales and marketing for a large insurance company. Jack, being fairly extroverted, was good at his job but was not enormously motivated or passionate about it. He was having fun at this stage in his life, with no great ambitions in his current career and knew he would naturally flourish in a big organisation.

He was going on workshops outside of his work hours. He completed courses in anatomy and physiology, sports massage and counselling because he was naturally interested in them. Jack had a few anxieties at work around presentations and procrastination but was able to distract himself and avoid situations that would trigger those uncomfortable feelings. These anxieties influenced what he thought he could do – unhealthy thoughts about himself affected the quality of work he did and what he thought he was capable of.

Time passed. Jack began to feel less happy and knew it was time for a change – but what? One day, while walking to work, he felt very depressed and was aware of his self-critical language: "You are an idiot", "You are rubbish", "You are not where you should be", "What a failure" and "You are not doing what you want." A stranger stopped him in the street and asked, "Are you all right?" It was a shock to Jack; he didn't think other people could see. He decided to get some help. A friend suggested he took the programme on personal development run at work. This course resonated with him and introduced him to the role that cognitive psychology, emotional responsibility and psychological education play in our lives.

This programme helped him to change his attitude. He no longer experiences bouts of depression and his work has improved. And he has stopped being judgemental – of himself and others.

Before he changed his self-beliefs, Jack held a belief that:

I must know what I want. I'm a failure and stupid.

Solution

Prior to this programme, Jack held the unhealthy self-damning belief "It's all crap; I am crap", provoking his depressive feelings. After he had joined the programme, he realised that "if it is to be, then it's up to me. I can stop the negative self-talk and feel different and do something different." It was at this time that the anxiety and fear left Jack.

He changed his self-talk and underlying self-belief; he stopped globally rating himself negatively and took responsibility for his thoughts, beliefs and actions.

His healthy belief was:

I prefer to know what I want but I do not have to. I am a fallible and worthwhile human being who has choices.

As he changed his beliefs about himself and the world, a window was beginning to open and he began asking himself, "What do I want?" Jack realised he no longer wanted his current job, although he was happier and performing better. He began to identify what was important to him (it was quite obvious, given his natural interests) and the values he wanted to live by. He looked at what he was doing and noticed the pattern of behaviour. He also remembered the personality test he took after graduation, suggesting he would be well suited to becoming a counsellor. So Jack decided to do more counselling courses, which eventually led to REBT. It resonated with him. He finally knew what he wanted as his mind was no longer preoccupied with negative thoughts and self-damning.

Obstacle 2: "Thinking about what I want is too much effort" and how to overcome it

As mentioned earlier, we tend to disturb ourselves by demanding comfort. When we insist that we should be comfortable at all times, we tend to avoid circumstances that we feel uncomfortable about. In this obstacle, it is the avoidance of the discomfort triggered by the effort of thinking. It is provoked by the general theme that:

Life must be easy, hassle-free and comfortable.

It provokes more specific beliefs about effort, difficulty and ease. For example:

- Thinking about what I want must not be difficult; that would be unbearable.
- Thinking about what I want must be easy for me or else I couldn't tolerate it.
- It must be easy and comfortable for me when I think about what I want; I could not stand it if it wasn't.

These lead to the inability to take this first step to explore what we want. Often we choose to remain as we are: it feels more comfortable. These beliefs trigger anxiety whenever you find things challenging or uncomfortable.

Demanding that you must feel comfortable or that you must find things easy (e.g. thinking, in this case) may lead to avoiding situations or tasks that are challenging. Many of us want comfort and ease at all times, and why not? And yet there are many times in life when we find life and tasks challenging or uncomfortable but do not give up or refuse to do those things. Feeling discomfort and experiencing challenges is part of human existence. Indeed, when we get through the discomfort we tend to experience a sense of satisfaction. The stoic philosopher Epictetus discussed the concept of control. It is helpful for us to understand what is in our control, for example our thoughts, and what we are not in control of, like the weather, and the experiences that are somewhat in our control, such as driving a car. You may have come across this concept before: Alcoholics Anonymous has enshrined it in its "The Serenity Prayer", which is based on Epictetus's philosophy.

 Reality Check

Holding the unhealthy belief "Thinking about what I want must be easy for me or else I can't tolerate it" is not consistent with reality. If it were true then no one would ever struggle with their thoughts if they ever thought about what they wanted. There is no universal law that states we must find thinking about what we want easy and effortless.

Common Sense

It doesn't make sense to demand that thinking about what you want be easy just because you'd like it to be so. It is understandable that you find thinking challenging. It requires mental effort. This part is true, but it makes no sense to then demand that it be easy.

Helpfulness

To insist that you must be in a state of effortless ease when you think about what you want is unhelpful to you. It provokes anxiety, negative thoughts and avoidance, which ultimately leads to you giving up on the first small step towards attaining your overall goal.

Low Frustration Tolerance (LFT)

LFT is a belief that underestimates your ability to cope with an adverse event and is often expressed as: "It is intolerable", "I can't cope", "I can't stand it" or "It is too hard."

This is an LFT belief that "Thinking about what I want must not be difficult, that would be unbearable. Thinking about what I want must be easy for me or else I can't tolerate it." It underestimates your ability to cope and would lead to avoidance of the step.

 **Reality Check**

Holding an unhealthy belief that you must find thinking about what you want easy and comfortable and if you don't then you can't stand it is not based in reality. You experience difficulties and challenges without falling to pieces. You may not like it. You may find thinking about what you want an effort, and yet it just isn't true that you can't stand it.

 **Common Sense**

You may find thinking about what you want an effort and difficult. This is fine. Believing that because it is an effort it is something you can't stand doesn't make sense. Although thinking about this is a challenge, it does not follow that it is intolerable or unbearable.

(☺) **Helpfulness**

It doesn't help you to believe that you can't tolerate thinking about what you want because it is not easy. Having such an LFT to thinking

19

about what you want provokes a negative attitude. You may end up doing something that was easy and comfortable in the short term but you would have also given up on your important goal. It leads to short-term comfort and long-term discomfort. Beliefs that support us through things that we find difficult enable long-term goal achievements.

Case study: David – I must be able to do things without effort

David finished university with an average degree after a rather excellent school career. He found schoolwork very easy. After university he took odd low-paid jobs, worked and partied hard. He was dissatisfied with his life but found he could not make the effort to think about what he wanted. He used alcohol to anaesthetise his feelings and bemoaned his lot.

David had LFT to the effort of thinking about change. During school, he was easily the top of his class and very competent at most sports and made the "A" team for most activities. He was well thought of by his teachers, peers and family. Everyone believed that he was destined for "great things". If something did not come easily to him, he looked to avoid it.

His unhealthy belief was about insisting that all things must come easily to him. For example:

I must always be able to do things without effort. I can't stand it if they don't come easily.

The above belief was a general one that was triggered by anything he found challenging, including thinking about the changes he wished to make.

For David, holding unhealthy beliefs of demanding that things must happen without effort continues to support his dysfunctional avoidant behaviours. It is unrealistic to think that things should happen without effort (including thinking) or that things should be easy. There is no evidence to support this belief. It will continue to be unhelpful to him. He believes that thinking about what he should do should be easy for him. He is unprepared to apply himself to making any progress on finding out what he wants in life, while still bemoaning his misfortune.

Solution

For David to begin to change his attitudes and behaviour he will have to repeat consistently and with force and vigour the healthy belief of:

I strongly prefer to do things without effort (including thinking about what I want) but I don't have to. I can stand it if things don't come easily, even though I don't like it.

By repeating this belief while beginning to explore what he may want to do, David will slowly begin to feel more able to engage with change as he develops a high frustration tolerance to making an effort. As David applies his healthy belief to the process of discovering what he wants and finds he can tolerate the challenge of this type of thinking discomfort, he will become increasingly confident with each attempt. The important change will be for David to consider what he wants to do and then writing that down. Without taking any action, nothing will change for David. In David's case he may find it helpful to sit with friends (probably over a couple of beers) and begin exploring ideas with their help before going on to develop these ideas on his own. Building resilience to difficulty and effort increases our confidence and helps us make the necessary steps to successfully complete our goals.

When we set up the College and developed our company, City Minds, we spent many hours exploring what we wanted, how we wanted things to be, threw many ideas around, wrote and rewrote ideas with much debate over coffee and cake before working out our vision for both organisations. At times, we found it quite a struggle, but you just take a short break and get back to it.

Finally, once you have discovered after reflecting and exploring just what it is you want in your life, you are ready to move to the next stage: Step 2 – Gather information.

Exercise

1. Identify the unhealthy beliefs that are sabotaging you identifying what you want.
2. Question the unhealthy beliefs by using the following three checks:
>   Reality check.
>   Common sense.
>   Helpfulness.
3. Write the healthy belief down.
4. Identify the unhelpful excuses that maintain your unhealthy beliefs.
5. Identify the unhelpful behaviours that maintain your unhealthy beliefs.
6. List the benefits of achieving the goal.
7. Identify the helpful behaviours to achieve this step.
8. Mentally rehearse the healthy belief and take action while feeling uncomfortable.
9. Repeat, repeat, and repeat with consistency and force.
10. Take action while feeling uncomfortable.

Tips for Step 1: Identify What You Want

- If you find yourself avoiding the step, check what you are thinking each time you attempt to begin and identify your unhealthy belief. Challenge the unhealthy belief and repeat your healthy preference belief in its place.
- Choose a goal that is important or significant to you. It is important on this first step, as you explore what you want, to choose something that you feel passionate about or that is significant to you.
- Write it down and put reminders in your environment, for example on the fridge door, in your diary or on your screen saver.
- This step is about beginning to aspire towards and to be inspired about something. There is no particular time limit.
- Visualise the goal regularly.

"We are the creative force of our life, and through our own decisions rather than our conditions, if we carefully learn to do certain things, we can accomplish those goals."

Stephen Covey

Step 2

Gather Information

"Knowledge is of two kinds. We know a subject ourselves, or we know where we can find information on it."
Samuel Johnson

Gathering information, or fact finding, is the second step after you have identified what you want. If you already have enough information about what you want then you can skip to Step 3 (Set achievable goals), but if you want to continue reading then you may gain further understanding of how CBT can be used to solve problems about gathering information.

Gathering information is about finding the relevant information about what you wish to achieve or about what you are interested in. It can help in a number of ways:

- You can utilise your time more efficiently and effectively.
- You can develop new skills, such as learning to think critically, by sifting and sorting through the information.
- You may broaden your outlook and gain inspiration.
- People gather information for many reasons and from a wide variety of sources.

There are many different sources of information available to you, including:

- Books.
- Newspapers.
- The Internet.

- Audio/videotapes.
- Your own knowledge and experience.
- Family members, friends and colleagues.
- Reports.
- Surveys.
- Policy statements from government.
- Industry.
- Commerce.
- Professional bodies.
- Charities.
- Voluntary organisations.
- Academic institutions.
- Local government departments.

Start by thinking about what information you want and why. You may want to think in the ways outlined in the examples below.

Example 1: Gather information – Training to be a CBT therapist

What do I need the information for?

- To learn about the subject matter more.
- To find out what the required qualification is.
- To know how long training will last.
- To discover my earning potential.
- What does it involve?
- To find out about starter courses.

Example 2: Gather information – Marketing and selling a product you have invented

What do I need the information for?

- To check whether there is another product out there.
- To check for similar ideas.
- Is there a patent on it?
- How do I get a product patented?
- What is the market size?
- To develop a prototype.
- To work out development costs.

You can gather information about almost anything, from effective weight-loss strategies and becoming psychologically healthy to starting a social project, setting up your own business or getting involved in a humanitarian cause. The information is out there and there is a lot of it, too.

You may come across interesting information and other sources of information that you may not have anticipated. This can be useful but it can also expose you to contradictory information. It is a good idea to sift through the information and the opinions you have come across and think if it is:

- Directly relevant to what you want;
- Partially relevant or;
- Just irrelevant.

Stick to your guidelines and prioritise accordingly. The simplest question to ask yourself is: "Is this information really about what I want?"

The objective of Step 2 is to gather information about what you have decided you want to do.

As we have discussed in the "How to use this book", this book is about making small steps to achieve bigger things. Each step in this book is effectively a goal, and part of a process of working towards the overall goal to achieve what you want. If you have decided to gather information but are failing to do it or have given up, there is a reason for that. The reason is usually to do with feeling anxious at the thought of gathering information or when fact finding.

Obstacles to Step 2: Gather Information

People avoid or give up during this step because of the following obstacles:

1. Gathering information is too much like hard work and dull.
2. Gathering the information has now made me realise it is not what I want (i.e. I'm now unclear about what I want to achieve, once again).
3. I wonder whether it is really the right time in my life to start on this because of health, family or other priorities.
4. Gathering information means committing yourself to doing something afterwards.

When you set a goal, even if it is a small goal, that takes you a step closer to your ultimate goal, you become aware of:

- Your current reality, which is familiar or comfortable and;
- Your goal.

In this case, your current reality and the goal of completing the fact find. If you are not fact finding or have abandoned it, just reflect on what you feel at the thought of gathering information or during it. Are you in state of discomfort or anxiety?

29

When we feel anxious we tend to avoid the tasks that we have set ourselves or we tend to give up, ultimately failing to achieve our goals. We can also become very creative at justifying to ourselves that avoiding the task or giving up before we complete it is in our best interest. We rationalise our reason or reasons to not finish the task, putting a positive spin on avoidance and on giving up the goal.

Obstacle 1: "Gathering information is too much like hard work and dull" and how to overcome it

Avoiding or giving up on gathering information because it's too much like hard work and dull is provoked by holding an unhealthy belief about hard work and boredom. The unhealthy belief will take the form of the following general theme:

Life must be easy, comfortable and effortless.

The above attitude will give rise to many offshoot beliefs, as well as specific beliefs, such as:

- Gathering information must not be too hard to do and must not be dull. It's intolerable when it is.
- Gathering information must be effortless and not dull. It's intolerable when it isn't.
- Gathering information must be easy and not boring. It's intolerable when it isn't.

The above demands cannot be met if you are someone who finds gathering information too much of an effort and dull because you do not accept the fact that for you it is too much like hard work and dull. The problem of avoidance is not provoked by the fact that gathering information is too much like hard work and dull, but by the demand that it must not be so. If it's too much of an effort and dull, so be it. You have every right to find it so, but you don't have to give up. You can accept that, for you, gathering information is too much of an effort and dull and still do it anyway.

✓ Reality Check

There is no universal law that stipulates that life has to be easy, comfortable and effortless. This also applies to the specific belief about gathering information. There is no universal law that stipulates that it must not be too hard and that it must not be dull. Gravity is a universal law. It always exists on planet earth. If such a universal law existed about hard work and boredom, every human being would never experience work that was too much like hard work and no one would ever experience boredom or find anything dull. But we all do find some tasks that are too much of an effort and we all find some tasks dull and boring too. Effort and boredom cannot be avoided, and demanding that we must not experience them does not stop them from being part of our reality. Avoiding them can lead us to give up on important goals.

💭 Common Sense

It is understandable to want certain tasks to be easier and exciting. After all, who would deliberately choose dull tasks? Wanting work to be on the right side of effort and wanting it to be interesting is one thing, but just because it is how you like it to be doesn't follow that it must be so. Demanding what you desire from life does not make sense. What would you say to someone who thinks like this? *I want the day to be nice, sunny and cool every day and because this is what I want it must be so.* It is easy to grasp how illogical and absurd this is, yet it is based on the same illogical premise that the demand for gathering information not to be too much like hard work and dull is founded on.

 **Helpfulness**

The belief gathering information must not be too much like hard work and dull is unhelpful. The demand would provoke anxiety at the thought of gathering information. It would provoke all sorts of thoughts to convince yourself to either delay it or to do something else. You will tend to choose to do other tasks that require less effort or tasks that are more enjoyable, but ultimately it sabotages what you have deemed as an important part of your plan that moves you a step closer to your overall goal – the goal you identified in Step 1.

Low Frustration Tolerance (LFT)

LFT is a belief that underestimates your ability to cope with an adverse event and is often expressed as: "It is intolerable", "I can't cope", "I can't stand it" or "It is too hard."

In this case, you may feel that gathering information must be easy and that, if it's not, it's intolerable.

 **Reality Check**

It is completely untrue that you cannot tolerate hard work. You will not explode if you do hard work and you certainly do not explode when you do dull work either. To believe that you cannot stand gathering information because it too much like hard work and dull would imply that the moment you thought about it you would explode, but clearly that doesn't happen. You do tolerate it and you do stand it but you find it difficult and frustrating.

Common Sense

Acknowledging that you find hard work and dull work frustrating and difficult is fine; believing that because it is frustrating it is intolerable doesn't make sense. It does not follow that just because something is frustrating and an effort it is intolerable or unbearable.

Helpfulness

It doesn't help you to believe that hard work and dull work are intolerable. For a start, this attitude would provoke anxiety just when you think about the task at hand (i.e. gathering information). The LFT belief also provokes you to find creative ways to sidetrack yourself from "sitting put and getting on with the work". It will provoke you to tend to do something "nicer", "more enjoyable" and "less of an effort", and will defocus you from your overall goal. You may end up doing something that was more comfortable in the short term but you would have also given up on your important goal.

Case study: Ella – It must be interesting

Ella works for a large company, in the marketing department. She wants to become a senior product development executive in the next five years and has ambitions to become a marketing manager too. She has been motivated about all the marketing projects that have involved creative work such as briefing and working with design and advertising agencies. She has been asked to gather information about some technical compliance issues concerning a particular project. She has been avoiding this task because she holds the belief that:

My work must be interesting and enjoyable to me. I cannot stand working on boring things like compliance.

As a consequence of this belief, Ella has been getting anxious because she knows that she is required to fact find some compliance issues while delaying and putting off doing anything about it. She starts the day with good intentions but as soon as she thinks about doing this work she feels anxious and uncomfortable and starts to think the following:

- I'm not interested in compliance. Why me? I like marketing – not this.
- I hate thinking and reading about compliance. It's so boring. I can't stand reading anything about it.
- I can't concentrate on reading about compliance. I just can't do it.
- My mind shuts down just thinking about it.
- I have time, I'll do something else now and have another go later.
- I wonder if I can ask someone else to do it. My manager won't be impressed, though.
- How can I get out of doing this? I hate this.

Ella then continues to avoid doing the work. She has started to moan and gossip about what she has been asked to do. She jumps to help anyone who asks for her opinion and guidance just to get away from working on the compliance fact find. Her anxiety is getting worse as her manager has asked her a few times about how she is getting on with the fact finding.

Ella's thoughts and behaviour are provoked by her unhealthy belief that:

My work must be interesting and enjoyable to me. I cannot stand working on boring things like compliance.

Solution

Ella would achieve the task by challenging her demand and by understanding that, while she would love to always work on interesting and enjoyable tasks, sometimes this might not be the case and that she could tolerate this even though she didn't like it. She could certainly stand her frustration even if she found it difficult. She would not fall to pieces or explode while fact finding about compliance. She would also stop the moaning and gossiping and not distract herself from doing her job by getting herself too involved in other people's less boring work. She would forcefully recite the following healthy belief and sit with her discomfort as she did fact finding:

It would be preferable if my work was always interesting and enjoyable but it does not have to be. While I find boring tasks frustrating and difficult, I can tolerate them and do them.

This healthy belief is helpful to Ella as it would provoke the right type of discomfort (i.e. not anxiety) and help her to take constructive action. She would perform her task, act professionally and increase the likelihood of striving for her ambitions. She would also develop resilience, helping her see that she can cope and achieve even when she finds things frustrating.

Obstacle 2: "Gathering the information has now made me realise it is not what I want (i.e. I'm now unclear about what I want to achieve, once again)" and how to overcome it

Sometimes we can get excited about a new idea or realisation, even having an "ah-ha" moment when things become clear and we become motivated about what we want. It's not unusual to have these moments or even periods of clarity about a new idea or a new goal. The natural thing is to then start talking about it with friends. Our ears prick up when we hear or see something about it or associated with it. What can also happen though, is that you may begin to realise that this goal may not be what you want after all.

You may have, for example, had an idea about buying a timeshare flat or perhaps thought about doing a degree in sports psychology, particularly after watching the Olympics. You feel excited about this new prospect and what the future holds for you. You start gathering information from the Internet, reading about it and so on. Slowly you start to realise it is not for you and you are back to square one, not knowing what you want. The thought of taking time and thinking and reflecting again provokes anxiety because you are once again unclear about what you want to achieve.

This is not unusual. In fact, it happens to all of us at some point or another. Accept it, but don't give up on your search. You can go back to Step 1 (Identify what you want) and start again.

The unhealthy belief will take the form of the following general theme:

I must achieve what I expect of myself.

37

The above attitude will give rise to many offshoot beliefs as well as specific beliefs, such as:

- I must be clear and sure about what I want to achieve all the time.

This demand may have any of the three potential derivative beliefs or any of their combinations as follows:

- The fact that I'm not clear about what I want to achieve is unbearable (LFT).
- The fact that I'm not clear about what I want to achieve is awful (awfulising).
- The fact that I'm not clear about what I want to achieve proves I'm useless (self-damning).

✓ Reality Check

The demand "I must be clear and sure about what I want to achieve all the time" is plainly unrealistic. There's no universal law that stipulates any one of us must be clear about what we want to achieve all the time. If such a law existed then you would not find one person who was unclear about what they wanted to achieve. Clearly, this demand is unrealistic, and ignores the fact that many of us are often unclear about what we want to achieve.

Common Sense

It is completely natural to desire and wish for clarity about what we want to achieve all the time, but it doesn't make sense to turn this wish or desire into a dogmatic demand. Turning your desires into dogmatic demands is at the heart of your problem.

 **Helpfulness**

It really doesn't help to internally demand that you must be clear about what you want to achieve all the time. This demand provokes anxiety and a tendency to avoid. In such a state you are more likely to give up on the small step that is part of a bigger goal. You do not get any long-term returns from holding such a belief. You will feel a short-term or momentary relief but that's about it . . . and then straight back to having the same problem again.

Low Frustration Tolerance (LFT)

LFT is a belief that underestimates your ability to cope with an adverse event and is often expressed as: "It is intolerable", "I can't cope", "I can't stand it" or "It is too hard."

In this case, you may think, "I must be clear about what I want to achieve all the time – if I'm not, I can't stand it."

 **Reality Check**

Believing that lack of clarity is unbearable (LFT) is also erroneous. What's the evidence that you cannot bear lack of clarity? Does your brain permanently shut down when you are unclear? Do you explode into a million pieces the moment you lack clarity? Of course not. Your brain still works and you still breathe, which proves that you can bear it.

 **Common Sense**

You may say, yes, but I really find it frustrating and difficult, I really don't like being unclear about what I want to achieve. You'd be right.

It is frustrating, it is difficult and you don't like it – but you are still bearing it. Which of the two beliefs is the more realistic, logical and helpful:

- I can't bear being unclear about what I want to achieve, or;
- It's hard and frustrating but not unbearable being unclear about what I want to achieve?

Helpfulness

The first belief above is unhelpful because it provokes anxiety, negative thoughts and avoidance, which ultimately lead to you giving up on the small step towards your overall goal. It stops you from having clarity because your mind will focus on the fact that you are not clear, as opposed to exploring and looking for clarity.

Awfulising

Awfulising is an unhealthy/irrational belief that when a demand is not fulfilled the badness is viewed as 100% or more bad (i.e. end-of-the-world bad, nothing else is worse in that moment). It is often expressed as: "It is a disaster", "It is awful/terrible/horrible", "It is a catastrophe" or "It is the end of the world."

Reality Check

Awfulising in this instance is about making lack of clarity the worst thing that could happen, 100% or more bad. When you think about it, is there any evidence to support such a viewpoint? You really can't think of anything worse than lacking clarity?

Common Sense

You may view lack of clarity as bad and that's fair enough but just because it is bad as far as you are concerned does not mean that it's awful (i.e. 100% bad). That wouldn't make sense. Keep it bad – but take the horror out of it.

Helpfulness

Viewing it as awful provokes anxiety, negative thoughts and avoidance, which will ultimately sabotage your progress. Your mind will once again be preoccupied with the fact that you are unclear as opposed to focusing in a calmer manner on continuing your reflection and figuring out what you want.

Self-damning

Self-damning is an unhealthy/irrational and wholly negative judgement of oneself based on the non-fulfilment of a demand. Often expressed as, "I'm worthless", "I'm not good enough", "I'm a failure" or "I'm stupid" and so on.

It is understandable and very human to look at your friends or colleagues and compare your lot with theirs. Most people start with this comparison and then end up making themselves feel worse. The problem isn't with the act of making a comparison but with the conclusion you make about yourself following that comparison. You may compare job titles, salary, intelligence, looks or knowledge and so on. In this case, you may know someone who has been clear and sure about what they wish to achieve in their life all the time. It could be a friend, brother, sister or a colleague. Indeed, some people are clear and sure from a young age for all sorts of reasons. Of course, it's reasonable to want the same clarity, but if you don't then that's the reality right now. You are not a useless person because, right here and now, you don't possess clarity.

✓ Reality Check

Believing that you are useless for not having clarity about what you want to achieve all the time is just not right. There's no evidence to prove that you are useless. You are a complex human being with both psychological and biological traits. You think, you have feelings, you have memories and you have skills. You will have strengths and weaknesses just like everyone one else. Not having clarity about what you want to achieve all the time does not negate all your other aspects, which in reality you cannot even list as there are so many of them.

Common Sense

You may view this lack of clarity as a failing and it is fine to view it in that way, but this specific failing does not make you a useless person. Many people make this part/whole error. They take one particular aspect they deem is failing and then damn themselves totally because of it. Does this sound like good sense to you?

Helpfulness

If you continued to make this part/whole error (i.e. continued to put yourself down as useless or in some other self-damning way), just reflect on the benefits that you are getting from thinking in this way about yourself. Does it help you succeed and achieve the tasks and goals you have in mind? Does it help you feel good about yourself? Does it help you take constructive actions at all? Unlikely, as you will spend your time beating yourself up and recalling other past failures and finding even more reasons to prove to yourself that you are useless. Time well spent? Remember that this way of thinking is a consequence of holding a self-damning belief.

Case study: Martin – I must know what I want

Martin is a 40-year-old man. He has worked throughout his teenage and adult life but has never found anything he truly wanted to do. For the last four years he has been working in a bank. He does his job, is good at it and at the end of the day he goes home to his family. He is not unhappy but he wants to find something that he enjoys or has some passion about. One of the things that Martin has regretted is not going to university to study ancient history, which was something he enjoyed when he was younger. He has talked about this with his wife and decided he will start looking at this option. When he starts to gather information about university courses, he realises that he really doesn't want to become a student again and doesn't really want to study ancient history. He then stops gathering information about courses on ancient history and becomes frustrated. He gets anxious when he has another idea or when his wife suggests an idea for him because he holds the unhealthy belief "I must know what I want."

He has been avoiding fact finding or exploring new ideas because he holds the belief that:

I must become clear and sure about what I want to achieve all the time. If not, it's unbearable, awful and proves I'm useless.

This belief provokes anxiety at the thought of fact finding a new idea and he avoids it. It provokes thoughts along the following lines:

- Knowing me, I'll have a doubt.
- What's the point of it? I'm 40.
- I may find out I hate it and then I'd have wasted money.
- I should know and shouldn't be thinking of new ideas at the age of 40.

- It's a silly idea and I'm sure nothing will come of it, so what's the point of fact finding?

Martin continues to explore many new ideas and dismisses them all, even when he initially gets excited by some of them. His thoughts and reactions are provoked by his internal insistence that he must be clear and sure.

Solution

Martin will free himself from being stuck by accepting the reality that at the moment he doesn't know and doesn't have certainty. He doesn't have to like it but he can accept this reality. It is bad but not the end of the world that he doesn't have clarity, and he can certainly stand this, even though it is frustrating. Not having clarity and certainty does not make him a useless person. It would be far more beneficial for him to accept himself unconditionally as opposed to putting himself down. The healthy belief for Martin is:

I want to be clear and sure about what I want all the time but I don't absolutely have to be. The fact that I'm not is bad but not the worst thing that could happen to me. It's frustrating, but I can bear it: it doesn't make me useless. I accept myself as I fallible person, and my worth doesn't depend on whether I'm clear and sure about what I want to achieve.

The above belief will help Martin become concerned rather than anxious. It will help take the pressure off him, helping him to focus on finding what he truly wants to do as opposed to focusing on the fact the he doesn't know what he wants to do. He will need to explore and fact find each idea, even if he decides to rule it out. This will help him to continue reflecting on what he wants and therefore increase the likelihood of finding it. He doesn't have to be absolutely clear and certain before he fact finds. The healthy mindset for Martin is to accept doubts and uncertainties and not allow them to become a reason for stopping himself from taking a small step forward.

Obstacle 3: "I wonder whether it is really the right time in my life to start on this because of health, family or other priorities" and how to overcome it

You may avoid gathering information because you question if it is the right time in your life to start. This may be because of health, family or other priorities and is provoked by holding an unhealthy belief that life conditions must be "just so" before you take any kind of action, including the small step of gathering information. It is provoked by the belief that has the following theme:

Life must be easy, comfortable, hassle-free and effortless.

The above general belief will have its specific offshoots, such as:

- Life conditions must be just so before I do something. If they are not, I won't be able to handle it.
- Life conditions must be perfect before I even think about doing what I want. If they are not, it would be awful.
- Everything has to be in balance before I strive for what I want. If not, I won't cope.

The above beliefs will stop you from even taking a simple step forward like fact finding. The interesting thing is that you don't have to do anything more beyond fact finding if you choose not to. You may also find out that taking this small step helps you to realise that you can go forward with your plans. Avoiding fact finding will remove these two options for you.

✓ Reality Check

If you think about the demands on life and its conditions, you will realise that there is no law of the universe that stipulates that life conditions must be just so, perfect or that you must not have other important priorities in your life. If such a universal law existed then we would only achieve tasks if life conditions were always just so. You can see that people still do things that they want to do even if their life conditions are not just so.

☁ Common Sense

Wouldn't it be lovely if life conditions were always perfect and in balance for all of us? That would be a good place to start working on achieving our goals, but it doesn't follow that life conditions must be just so, either. It's preferable but not essential.

☺ Helpfulness

Such demands put unhelpful pressure on you and sabotage your goals because they stop you from considering your options or being creative in finding alternative solutions. Holding such demands creates a very black-and-white mindset and you may not even see the options that actually exist. Such a belief would provoke tension and anxiety when you thought about fact finding a really interesting and potentially excellent idea. It would provoke a tendency to avoid thinking about the goal as well as exploring whether it was achievable. Ultimately, it would lead you to put it off, a decision you might regret were you to hear someone else doing something similar at a later date.

Awfulising

Awfulising is an unhealthy/irrational belief that when a demand is not fulfilled the badness is viewed as 100% or more bad (i.e. end-of-the-world bad, nothing else is worse in that moment). It is often expressed as: "It is a disaster", "It is awful/terrible/horrible", "It is a catastrophe" or "It is the end of the world."

In this case, you might think, "Life conditions must be perfect before I even think about doing what I want. If they were not, it would be awful."

 Reality Check

It is not awful when life conditions are not perfect. The world does not come to an end and there are worse things than imperfect life conditions. You can prove it. What would be worse than imperfect life conditions?

Common Sense

Of course, it makes sense that you want life conditions to be perfect. You may view this imperfection as bad or really bad, and we won't argue with you about that. We would ask, just because imperfect life conditions are bad, does it follow that they are awful? Awfulising badness does not make sense. Loading it with horror does not make sense.

Helpfulness

Viewing imperfect life conditions as awful is not only untrue and does not make sense: it is also unhelpful. This view provokes anxiety whenever you want to do something and you think that your life conditions are not perfect. It destabilises you and leads to your avoiding taking a simple step. It provokes a tendency to run away, ultimately stopping you from even completing fact finding.

Exercise

Using the reality check, common sense and helpfulness arguments, ask yourself, "Why is believing that I won't be able to handle it if life conditions are not perfect an irrational or unhealthy belief?"

Case study: Juliet – My life conditions don't have to be perfect

This case study is an examination of how a change in attitude and self-belief can affect what you are able to achieve. Juliet always knew what she wanted to do. She wanted to become a therapist. She couldn't find a path to do it. The path to it required long training and low pay initially. She was told by her father from an early age, "You have to support yourself and be independent." After university she went into business, all the time knowing that she wanted to be in the psychological world. She considered human resources but chose finance, purely for the money. "I was adequate and made a pretty good living but wasn't feeling it," she said.

At 26/27, she was doing voluntary work and going to work. She eventually got married and had one child. When he went to school, she wanted to return to work doing something she really wanted to do. She started her psychological training. Then she had a second child, followed by her husband leaving. She stopped her studies and went back to finance. She became a single parent but still wanted to continue with her retraining. After two years, she resumed her studies. She wondered how much she could earn when she qualified. She said,

"I could have said this is not the right time in my life but didn't. I didn't because I changed my belief about myself."

Before she changed her self-beliefs, Juliet had two anxiety-provoking beliefs:

I must support myself financially at all costs. If I can't, something awful will happen.

I must be good enough. If I am not, I am useless.

Solution

Both of Juliet's beliefs were influenced by her upbringing. She was told "You're useless" by her family and her father had told her, "I love your mother, then your brother and lastly you." In that order. He had told her that when she was in her twenties and to her it made sense because first came the mother, then the brother and then she was born. She said, "I did feel I was loved last but I didn't know why. When he told me in my twenties, I thought, 'Now you're telling me the truth because it wasn't true that we were loved equally.' I could accept that."

Being a single mother, she realised that she could manage on her own and learnt to challenge the belief that she was useless. She was supporting herself and her children. She believed she was adequate (some said very good) at her job. She wasn't perfect, but neither was she useless. She changed her beliefs because she realised the world did not come to an end when she struggled financially: she was able to adapt and think of solutions. Her situation was not ideal. She would have preferred life to have been easier. She would have preferred not being a single parent. She would have preferred her life circumstances to have been different. They weren't. They did not have to be for her to start retraining either. She started to fact find new courses despite the fact that her life circumstances were not ideal. This time she did so, but without anxiety. She felt confident because of her healthy beliefs and because she had overcome challenges and learnt from them. This set her up for success in pursuit of her goal. Conditions did not have to be perfect.

Obstacle 4: "Gathering information means committing yourself to doing something afterwards" and how to overcome it

Gathering information is just one step out of a few that can help you get closer to achieving what you want. Avoiding this task because it implies you have to commit to doing something afterwards is provoked by an unhealthy belief about commitment to take action. The unhealthy belief will take the form of the following general theme:

I must achieve what I expect of myself.

The belief will give rise to many offshoot beliefs as well as specific ones, such as:

- I have to take action once I complete gathering information. If I don't, it proves I'm useless.
- I have to commit to achieving my goal once I have completed the fact find. If I didn't, it would be terrible and would prove I was a failure.
- I have to keep going and do something after I gather information. If I didn't, it would be unbearable and prove that I was lazy and weak.

✓ Reality Check

The above demands are not consistent with reality. You do not have to do anything after you gather information. Where is it written that you have to take action, make a commitment or keep going? It's not a universal law. No one would be holding a gun to your head if you stopped having completed a fact find. It's just a step. You can complete it, but you don't have to do anything more afterwards. If it were a universal law that you had to make a commitment to take action or to achieve your goal after the fact find then you would find that everyone in the world would be doing that automatically. The possibility of not doing something afterwards would not exist. Everyone would always take action after they gathered information about something of interest. You can observe that this is not the case. You can indeed choose to do something afterwards but you can also choose to delay taking action or not bother at all. It is simply not something that you have to do afterwards.

 Common Sense

You could be thinking, "Well, in that case, what's the point of gathering information if I don't take action afterwards?" The point is based on the fact that there is a difference between wanting to and choosing to do something and making a demand that you have to. Demanding that you have to take action does not make sense.

Just because you may want to take action after you complete the fact find doesn't mean that you absolutely have to. Think about the following two beliefs:

- I want to take action after I gather information, but it doesn't mean that I absolutely have to.
- I want to take action after I gather information and therefore I absolutely have to.

Which belief is logical and makes sense?

You don't have to take action, you don't have to commit to taking action and you don't have to keep going. You may want to, like to and choose to take action – but you certainly don't have to.

 Helpfulness

If you kept making the demand that you have to do something or you have to take action afterwards, you would feel anxiety and you would tend to avoid doing the fact find. Your mind would be preoccupied with having to take action when in fact all you needed to do would be to gather some information about what you were interested in. That's it. The demand to achieve the goal or to take action will sabotage this simple step. The demand stops you from feeling that you have a choice, when in fact you do. Letting go of it frees you and focuses your mind on your goal. You would not feel as if someone was holding onto your belt while you were trying to walk. If you took the demand out of your desire to do something, you would do it more successfully. This is because you would feel motivated to take action, as opposed to feeling coerced into taking action. Constructive motivation is based on choice and desire, as opposed to coercive motivation, which is based on the "I have to do it or else" attitude.

Self-damning

Self-damning is an unhealthy/irrational and wholly negative judgement of oneself based on the non-fulfilment of a demand. Often expressed as, "I'm worthless", "I'm not good enough", "I'm a failure" or "I'm stupid" and so on.

In this case, you might think, "If I fail to take action after fact finding, it means I'm not good enough and a failure."

✓ Reality Check

Believing that you are a useless person for not taking action afterwards is erroneous. This is a self-damning belief. Many people rate themselves in this global way and believe that they are bad, weak, worthless and incompetent and so on if they fail at something (in the above examples, if they fail at taking action, committing to achieving a goal or to keep going with something they started). Basically, many people rate themselves totally if some condition they are demanding that they must fulfil is not met.

A self-damning belief is rigid and inconsistent with reality. When you label yourself as weak, then that's it: you have deleted all your strengths. When you label yourself as useless, you delete everything that you have been good at. You are believing in something that says this is how you always are, no room for change, no other qualities apart from "useless", "weak" and "lazy". Is this true? There is no evidence for this. Like all of us, you have strengths, weaknesses, you succeed, you fail, you like and dislike, love, feel positive emotions and negative emotions and a million and one other things. How would all the things that make you who you are disappear so that you became a totally weak person if you did not take action? They don't disappear. Think about it another way: if you became a useless person as a consequence of not taking action then from that moment onwards everything you did, said and thought would be useless. Nothing apart from uselessness would exist.

 ## Common Sense

It doesn't make sense to rate yourself in this black-and-white way based on the non-fulfilment of a demand. It doesn't make sense to think that if you don't take action or commit to your goal then everything about you becomes useless, weak or lazy. It doesn't follow logically to judge yourself in this global way because of a specific failing.

🙂 Helpfulness

If an evidence-based argument or common sense doesn't persuade you to see the flaw in a self-damning belief, then we would ask you to reflect on how helpful or pragmatic it is for you to continue maintaining and believing that you are useless, lazy and weak if you did not take action, commit to a goal or keep going. Does putting yourself down help you to succeed at taking action and achieving your goals in a healthy and constructive way? Or does believing that you are useless, weak and lazy fill your mind with negativity, leave you feeling anxious and unconfident? Do your putdowns help you to take action with confidence and success? Think about the consequences these beliefs have had and continue to have on you.

Awfulising

Awfulising is an unhealthy/irrational belief that when a demand is not fulfilled the badness is viewed as 100% or more bad (i.e. end-of-the-world bad, nothing else is worse in that moment). It is often expressed as: "It is a disaster", "It is awful/terrible/horrible", "It is a catastrophe" or "It is the end of the world."

How you view the badness of not fulfilling your demands can also be unhealthy for you in developing confidence and achieving success when you strive for your goals. Your feelings will give a clue as to how you are judging badness. With a belief like "I have to commit to achieving my goal once I complete the fact find. If I don't, it would be terrible and would prove I was a failure", badness is viewed not just as bad but terrible. In that moment, we believe that we will experience the worst-case scenario.

 **Reality Check**

Believing that a lack of commitment to the achievement of a goal would be terrible is dogmatic. Not committing to the achievement of the goal is judged as being 100% or more bad. It's a horror. This is unrealistic because worse things exist. The world would not come to an end if you did not commit to achieving your goal. The truth of the matter is that it would be bad or very bad but not terrible if you didn't. Surely you can think of worse things? Take the horror out of it.

 **Common Sense**

Consider the following two beliefs:

- It would be very bad if I didn't commit to achieving my goal, but it wouldn't be terrible.
- It would be very bad and therefore terrible if I didn't commit to achieving my goal.

Which of the above makes sense? We hope you said the first one. Of course, the first belief is logical: just because something is bad doesn't mean the world will end.

😀 **Helpfulness**

We have a choice in what we maintain as true. If a reality check and common sense arguments are still unpersuasive for you, take a moment to reflect on how holding a belief that it would be terrible (i.e. the worst thing that could happen that moment) if you didn't commit to achieving your goal is helpful to you. If you made an investment, you would look to gain some returns from it. How does viewing the badness in such an extreme and dogmatic way benefit you? It actually provokes anxiety. In a state of anxiety, you would tend to create even more negative possibilities in your head as well as withdraw from the task both mentally and physically. Ultimately, it stops you from completing something as simple as gathering information. You would have given up at the second hurdle, instead of jumping over it and moving forward to the next step. As a consequence, it feeds your feelings of lacking confidence and gives you further ammunition to beat yourself up with.

Low Frustration Tolerance (LFT)

LFT is a belief that underestimates your ability to cope with an adverse event and is often expressed as: "It is intolerable", "I can't cope", "I can't stand it" or "It is too hard."

 **Reality Check**

To believe that you cannot bear it if you don't keep going after you have completed the fact find is a complete exaggeration of reality and a huge underestimation of your ability to handle the frustration. You will feel frustrated if you don't keep going. You may find it difficult if you don't keep going, but you won't collapse in a heap.

Common Sense

It really doesn't make sense to exaggerate the difficulty of not taking action after fact finding is completed. Reflect on the following two beliefs:

- It would be frustrating but not unbearable if I didn't keep going after I fact find.

- It would be so frustrating that I would not be able to bear it if I didn't keep going.

Which of these two beliefs makes sense? Just because you would find it difficult does not mean it would be unbearable.

☺ Helpfulness

An LFT belief such as "I can't bear it if I didn't keep going" is unhelpful because it provokes anxiety. In a state of anxiety, your thoughts would be preoccupied with worrying about the "what ifs" as opposed to focusing on the task at hand. You would become distracted and, as a consequence, would avoid completing what was necessary. Ultimately, the small step that takes you a little closer to your overall goal would be missed, giving you plenty of ammunition with which to make yourself less confident.

Case study: Bob – I must take action

Bob is a 45-year-old self-employed business consultant. In the last five years he has been working long hours to keep his head above water. His demanding and challenging work led to him giving up on exercising and developing unhealthy eating habits, grabbing a sandwich here and there and then bingeing when he finally gets home. He has also been enjoying his wine a little too much as well. As a result, he has put on at least an extra two and half stone. He feels heavy and unhealthy and wants to lose the extra weight by joining a gym and eating healthily. As he is conscious of not wanting to spend excessively on annual membership, he needs to find out about local gyms and their membership fees and the weekly costs of attending at least twice a week. However, he has been putting this simple task off. He gets anxious whenever he thinks about doing some fact finding.

He then quickly finds something else to do instead. Bob holds the belief that:

I absolutely have to take action and go to the gym once I find out which gym is best for me. Not taking action just proves that I'm lazy and a failure.

This belief will provoke anxiety whenever he thinks about looking for a suitable gym. It provokes negative thoughts, such as:

- What's wrong with me? Why am I so useless?
- I'll think about this tomorrow. I'm too tired now.
- You'll just fail. You're just lazy.
- Why can't I just do this? It's ridiculous.

Bob continues to put himself down for failing to do this simple task. His anxiety, avoidant behaviour and thoughts are provoked by his demand that he must take action afterwards.

Solution

Bob will free himself from his anxiety by adopting a healthy attitude and realising that he really doesn't have to do anything after completing the fact find. It's not a universal law that he must take action. It doesn't make sense to demand taking action and it actually stops him in his tracks. He also needs to accept himself unconditionally. Even if at times he behaves in a lazy manner, this lazy behaviour does not mean that he is a totally lazy human being. If he fails to take action and go to the gym, it doesn't mean he is a total failure either. He is a fallible person and his worth does not depend on whether he goes to the gym afterwards either. He will need to think in the following way:

I really want to take action and go to the gym after I find out which gym is best for me but I don't have to. If I don't go to the gym, it doesn't mean I am totally lazy and a failure. I am a fallible person and my worth doesn't depend on whether I go to the gym.

This belief will help Bob focus on taking action. It will provoke concern and tension when he doesn't take action but in that state he will focus back on what he wants to do (take action) more quickly. His mind will not be preoccupied with damning himself and making himself anxious. He won't be happy if he doesn't take action but he won't be anxious either. He will be in a healthy but negative state if he doesn't take action. This healthier state will help him to pursue his desire.

Exercise

1. Identify the unhealthy beliefs that are sabotaging your attempts to gather information.
2. Question the unhealthy beliefs by using the following three checks:
>   Reality check.
>   Common sense.
>   Helpfulness.
3. Write the healthy belief down.
4. Identify the unhelpful excuses that maintain your unhealthy beliefs.
5. Identify the unhelpful behaviours that maintain your unhealthy beliefs.
6. List the benefits of achieving this step.
7. Identify the helpful behaviours needed to achieve this step.
8. Mentally rehearse the healthy belief and take action while feeling uncomfortable.
9. Repeat, repeat and repeat with consistency and force.
10. Take action while feeling uncomfortable.

This chapter has been about gathering information and discussed how your unhealthy beliefs can become obstacles to your progress at this stage. We have illustrated these unhealthy beliefs and how to challenge them with the three major challenges of: reality testing, whether they make sense and if they are helpful to you. Below are some tips to help you stay focused towards your longer-term goal.

Tips for Step 2: Gather Information

- Set some time in your diary and start to gather information towards your goal. Commit to doing this.
- Focus on the relevant information only.
- Conditions may not be perfect in your life but all that you need do is fact find.
- You may decide that the project is not of interest to you, which is fine. Go back to Step 1 (Identify what you want).
- You don't have to allow doubts to stop you from gathering information.
- Actively gather information on a regular basis.
- Take time to review the information you gather.
- Remember that you are not committing to doing anything, other than fact find.

"It is a capital mistake to theorize before one has data."

Arthur Conan Doyle

Step 3

Set Achievable Goals

"The reason most people never reach their goals is that they don't define them, or ever seriously consider them as believable or achievable. Winners can tell you where they are going, what they plan to do along the way, and who will be sharing the adventure with them."
Denis Watley

Having gathered all the information about what you want, you will have begun to clarify just what you do, and do not, want to achieve. Goals are about what we really want and desire. Setting clear and strong goals that you can visualise triggers your creative subconscious to create the energy and creativity to reach the goal. We as humans are quite naturally goal-orientated; in our daily lives there is a sequence of mini goals – be it getting to work, what we want to achieve in each day, what we are going to eat – and longer-term goals – such as looking forward to a holiday, planning Christmas and so forth.

If you want to succeed, you set clear goals. Without goals, you lack focus and direction. Goal setting not only allows you to take control of your life's direction; it also provides you with a benchmark for determining whether you are actually succeeding. For example, having a million dollars in the bank is only proof of success if one of your goals is to amass riches. If your goal is to practise acts of charity, then keeping the money for yourself would be contrary to how you would define success: the goal would be how you charitably distributed the wealth.

To accomplish your goals you need to know how to set them. You cannot simply say, "I want" and expect it to happen. So Step 3 (Set achievable goals) is about how to set goals in the most efficient, clear way.

Goals can sometimes be too far away from where we are at present. You may ask, "How can I achieve it?" Cognitive psychology explains that, provided we can see the result clearly and provided that we are emotionally committed, we can achieve the goal. It is important to set goals that:

- Motivate you.
- Are SMART.
- You are able to visualise.

When you set goals for yourself, it is important that they motivate you: this means making sure that they are important to you and that there is value in achieving them. If you have little interest in the outcome, or they are irrelevant given the larger picture, then the chances of you putting in the work to make them happen are slim. Motivation is key to achieving goals. It is important that goals are based on constructive motivation as opposed to coercive motivation. Constructive motivation is based on personal values, desires and rewards. Coercive motivation is based on fears and "musts"; it is the "carrot" versus the "stick" approach.

The most achievable goals tend to relate to the high priorities in your life. Without this type of focus, you can end up with far too many goals, leaving you too little time to devote to each one. Goal achievement requires commitment to maximise the likelihood of success, choosing a single goal where you experience a sense of urgency and having a strong desire for the outcome is more likely to result in that goal being achieved. When you don't have this, you risk putting off taking the action to making the goal a reality because it is just not that important to you.

Exercise

To make sure your goal is motivating, write down why it's valuable and important to you. Ask yourself, "If I were to share my goal with others, what would I tell them to convince them it was a worthwhile goal?" You can use this motivating value statement to help you if you start to doubt yourself or lose confidence in your ability to actually make the goal happen.

SMART Goals

You have probably heard of "SMART" goals. But do you always apply the rule? The simple fact is that for goals to be powerful they are best when designed to be SMART. There are many variations of what SMART stands for, but the essence is this:

- Specific.
- Measurable.
- Attainable.
- Realistic.
- Time bound.

Specific Goals

Ensure your goal is clear and well defined. Vague or generalized goals are unhelpful because they don't provide sufficient direction. If you say I want to lose weight, get fitter, work harder, be more successful, these statements do not give a clear picture as to exactly what that means. Being specific is about identifying what "fitter" or "successful", for example, means. For some, it may mean being able to run for the bus without becoming breathless; for others it may be completing an "Iron Man" challenge. Goals show you the way. Make it as easy as you can to get where you want to go by defining precisely where you want to end up.

Measurable Goals

State specific amounts, dates and so on in your goals so you can measure your degree of success. If your goal is simply defined as "To cut down on expenditure", how will you know when you have been successful?

When you say you want to cut down on your expenses, you have to tell yourself by how much and within what timeframe. Without a way to measure your success, you miss out on the sense of success that comes with knowing you have actually achieved what you set out to do.

Attainable Goals

Make sure that it's possible to achieve the goals you set. Setting a goal that you have no hope of achieving will guarantee failure and may leave you vulnerable to disturbing yourself. If are unfit and over 50, it is unlikely that you will become an astronaut. So why set yourself up for that fall?

Goals that are too easy, on the other hand, can be unrewarding. Setting challenging yet realistic goals is a good balance, the degree of difficulty is achievable with effort and so you experience satisfaction on completion. For example, setting the goal that you wish to pay off a mortgage in one year when you have a £250,000 mortgage and you earn £30,000 per annum would be unachievable unless you buy lottery tickets and get very lucky. A realistic goal would be to draw up a savings plan that could reduce your mortgage in a set number of years based on a realistic appraisal of the amount you could save.

Realistic Goals

The most effective goals are congruent with reality. Unrealistic goals are less likely to be achieved. One of the most common initial goals we come across with our clients is the "I want to be happy" one. This goal is unrealistic: is it realistic to be happy at all times? No, in reality everyone experiences times of sadness or frustration during their lifetimes. Realistic goals are based on what is evidenced and can be tested in reality. It is unrealistic to set a goal to achieve a size 48-inch chest in the next three weeks when you have 40-inch chest. No matter how many protein drinks you take or visits to the gym you make, the desired goal is unrealistic. However, to increase your chest measurement in three months by 2 cm is more realistic.

Time Bound Goals

Goals that have clear timelines are effective. It maintains focus and motivation if you have a clear timeline. You can introduce critical points of achievement in the timeline to remind yourself you are on track. This enables you to enjoy small successes along the way. When you have a stated time to focus towards, your sense of urgency and energy is triggered and achievement will be far more likely.

Example 1: Set achievable goals – A timeline

- **Five-year goal:** Become manager.
- **Six-month goal:** Start on management training course.
- **One-month goal:** Sign up for the training course.
- **One-week goal:** Find out how to sign up for the training course.
- **Today's goal:** Call HR to make an appointment to discuss the training course.

As you can see from this example, breaking big goals down into smaller, more manageable goals makes it far easier to see how the goal will get accomplished and gives you a clear timeline.

Exercise: Writing down goals

The physical act of writing down a goal makes it real and tangible. You have no excuse for forgetting about it. As you write, use the word "will" instead of "would like to" or "may". For example, "I will reduce my expenditure by one-third this year" not "I would like to reduce my expenditure by one-third this year."

The first goal statement is deterministic and suggests you have chosen and committed to this action. The second lacks conviction and commitment when using the conditional. It implies an option, from which you are more likely to be sidetracked. For example, if you visualise, "I will get my tax return done", you get an image of submitting or posting it. If you do the same with "I may get my tax return done", you may get an image of lots of papers and experience a sense of cloudy confusion or anxiety.

Take time to write the SMART goal that is important to you.

Example: Set achievable goals – Being SMART

Write down your general goal.

"Become a recognised international festival blogger and create a handbook on world festivals."

Having thought about what you want, gathered the information and decided what your goal is, it is now time to create a SMART goal around the general goal.

Specific

Ask questions about exactly what you want: in the above example you would ask yourself questions such as:

Question: What does "recognised" mean and by whom would I be recognised?

Answer: Book in all good bookshops in major cities around the world. Major travel agents would use the book and blog as a reference.

Question: Who would read my blog and who is my audience?

Answer: The blog would be the main reference site for festival goers around the world.

Getting specific really helps you to refine exactly what you want in a clearly identified way. You may find you discard some previous ideas as you apply this process until you have a very clear compelling goal you can visualise easily.

Measurable

Question: How much income do I wish to receive? (And so how many books would you have to sell?)

Answer: Work out an income you want from your goal (include paying start-up costs).

Question: How many visits to my website would there be for success?

Answer: Having fact found you would have an idea as to how many views would be appropriate for each country you have identified as relevant to you.

Achievable

Question: Is this an achievable goal – is it possible?

Answer: Yes, in appropriate timeframe, I have done my fact finding and there is little competition in the field.

Realistic

Question: In reality, would this product/book be of interest to people?

Answer: From my fact finding I discovered that there are over 10 million people worldwide who go to festivals annually.

> *Question: Is it realistic, considering my current situation, that I can achieve this?*
> *Answer: I have created a situation that will support this goal.*
>
> **Time bound**
>
> *Question: Is the timeframe in which I want to achieve this goal possible?*
> *Answer: Most probably; however, it may need some adaptation as I progress through the steps.*
>
> Write the goals in a timeline, as illustrated in the above example.
>
> While developing your vision within the SMART model, you will begin to adapt it until you have a very clearly defined goal and set of subgoals. You may find that, as you question each stage of the SMART model, you don't end up where you began this process.

Obstacles to Step 3: Set Achievable Goals

Having completed the two previous steps, you are on track to achieving your goal. You have gathered all the information, perhaps having discussed your goal with friends or family. You may be experiencing a sense of excitement about working towards your goal, but somehow you are not able to carry out the vital step of goal setting. People avoid or give up during this step because of the following obstacles:

1. I don't know how to goal set.
2. It is too difficult and too much effort to goal set.
3. I no longer desire what I want.
4. Goal setting is a step closer to my taking action, which makes me feel anxious.

Obstacle 1: "I don't know how to goal set" and how to overcome it

When you begin to consider goal setting for the first time, you do so knowing that you have never attempted anything like this before. And so it would be quite natural not to know how to complete this step without reading and completing the exercises in the previous section. If, however, you find yourself putting off reading the chapter or not completing the exercises, it is possible you are holding an unhealthy irrational belief about not knowing how to goal set.

Unhealthy beliefs will be around the general theme of:

I must perform well or outstandingly at all times.

When you avoid this step, or find yourself giving up at this point, You may be holding irrational beliefs that include this unhealthy demand and the three possible derivative beliefs of awfulising, LFT and self-damning. It will look something like the following:

• I absolutely must know how to goal set. It is awful if I don't. I cannot stand it and it proves I am stupid.

When we make demands like the ones above we are not accepting the fact that it is acceptable to "not know" how to do something. Many of us hold an unhealthy irrational belief that we absolutely must know how to do something, regardless of whether we have learnt it or not. Just because other people know how to do it, whatever it is (in this case goal setting), we make an assumption that everyone knows how to do it and somehow you "should" know it too. There is a tendency to think along the following lines:

• It must be obvious. What's wrong with me? If I don't know how to do this, how will I ever succeed?

- I can't do this. I am stupid.
- What's the matter with me? Why don't I know how to do this?
- I don't how to do this, so now I will never be able to get what I want.

If you demand that you must know how to goal set before you have even learnt how to do this, it will lead to failing this task, which can then lead to further unhealthy beliefs about lack of achievement and being a failure. These beliefs tend to provoke unhealthy and negative emotions, such as anxiety and depression.

✓ Reality Check

When you hold unhealthy beliefs, one of the first things to do is to check whether that belief is based in reality. There is no universal law that states you must know how to do something without being taught how to do it. Further, no universal law states we have to perform well at all times or achieve something in our lifetimes. It does, however, appear that although learning may be explicit (information that is specifically learnt, e.g. driving a car) or implicit (information we absorb without paying attention, e.g. learning your native language) we generally cannot carry out tasks or actions we have not learnt. It is unrealistic to hold a demand that we can do something that we have no experience of or have never been shown how to do. Universal laws, such as the existence of gravity or the fact that the earth rotates around the sun, are immutable and unquestionable; the belief that you can do something first off without anyone showing you how to is not. If knowing how to do something were a universal law, we would all be born with a knowledge of everything and be able to talk, drive a car, tie a shoelace and goal set the moment we were born! The reality is we know how to do things when we have learnt or been taught how to do them.

Common Sense

It is quite natural when you see other people seemingly going through life with perfect ease that you want your life to be the same and just "know" how to do everything you could ever think of; after all, who wouldn't? However, wanting or desiring something is not the same as demanding that it must be so. It does not make sense that just because you want something, in this case "knowing how to", it must be so. Imagine a demand that everyone must know a particular ancient dialect of a language that only a few people speak and it is demanded that you know just because you want to even though you have not been taught it or exposed to it. It makes no sense. We often make demands upon ourselves that make no sense. When we apply a little scrutiny, we often realise how illogical these demands are.

Helpfulness

The demand "I must absolutely know how to goal set" when attempting to goal set is not helpful. Holding this belief would provoke anxiety and avoidant behaviour at any point through the process of goal setting. This avoidant behaviour or tendency to do so may well sabotage your chances of completing this important step of identifying clearly your chosen goal.

Awfulising

Awfulising is an unhealthy/irrational belief that when a demand is not fulfilled the badness is viewed as 100% or more bad (i.e. end-of-the-world bad, nothing else is worse in that moment). It is often expressed as: "It is a disaster", "It is awful/terrible/horrible", "It is a catastrophe" or "It is the end of the world."

In this case, with goal setting, awfulising beliefs can provoke feelings of anxiety and a tendency for avoidance. It inhibits you from achieving goal setting and of achieving your bigger goal, identified in Steps 1 and 2.

 ## Reality Check

Holding the belief "not knowing how to goal set is more than 100% bad, and is awful" when you consider the reality of the situation does not hold true. There is no evidence that when you don't know how to do something it is beyond bad, that it is awful. Of course, it is not great to "not know how to do something", especially when you can see others being able to do something you want to be able to do. In reality, it is not awful, though it may be uncomfortable and challenging.

 ## Common Sense

Does it make any sense? Holding the belief that you must know how to goal set and not knowing how to would be awful does not make sense. If you consider not knowing as bad does it follow that it is awful? Yes, view it as bad but stop disturbing yourself by exaggerating the badness and making it the end of the world. It is not.

 ## Helpfulness

Beliefs that are helpful to us support our wishes and goals. They support us to achieve what we want. Holding the belief that not knowing how to goal set is so bad that it is awful does not support us. It provokes anxiety, which leads to avoidant behaviour and stops us from learning how, in this instance, to goal set. Holding this belief is unhelpful.

Low Frustration Tolerance (LFT)

LFT is a belief that underestimates your ability to cope with an adverse event and is often expressed as: "It is intolerable", "I can't cope", "I can't stand it" or "It is too hard."

In this case, it is linked to the demand "I absolutely must know how to goal set." You experience thoughts that you cannot stand it, that it is unbearable and you cannot cope with not knowing how to goal set.

 Reality Check

Is there any evidence to substantiate this belief in the real world? There is no evidence to be found in the belief that you cannot stand not knowing how to goal set. You will not shatter into tiny pieces when you do not know how to goal set. You can tolerate not knowing how to goal set, and even though you may find it frustrating or irritating it does not mean because you do not know how to goal set you cannot tolerate the discomfort or cannot learn how to goal set.

Common Sense

Accepting that it is frustrating or irritating when you do not know how to goal set makes sense. Believing that you cannot tolerate not knowing how to goal set does not. It does not follow that it is unbearable or intolerable when you do not know how to do something, even if it is irritating or frustrating at first.

Helpfulness

It does not help you to believe that not knowing how to goal set is intolerable. For a start, this attitude would provoke anxiety just when you start to think about the task at hand (i.e. goal setting). When we hold an LFT belief that provokes anxiety we tend to avoid what we are anxious about. We find remarkably creative ways of avoiding what we are anxious about. Rather than tolerate not knowing and learning how to set goals, we focus on the fact that we don't know and then divert our attention to other tasks, such as cleaning or filling in a tax return.

Self-damning

Self-damning is an unhealthy/irrational and wholly negative judgement of oneself based on the non-fulfilment of a demand. Often expressed as, "I'm worthless", "I'm not good enough", "I'm a failure" or "I'm stupid" and so on.

Holding the unhealthy belief "I absolutely must be able to know how to goal set" can lead to the belief "Because I don't know how to goal set, I am stupid or not good enough." This self-damning belief can lead to feelings of hopelessness and worthlessness as we believe we are somehow "less than others". This global self-rating is something many people do when some condition they demand must be fulfilled is not.

 ## Reality Check

You are wrong if you demand to know how to goal set and if you do not you are stupid. This is a self-damning belief. When you globally rate yourself, you exclude all other evidence to the contrary. Global self-damning deletes all previous experiences or knowledge that will have included strengths, successes, weaknesses and failures. This labelling of the self is not based on reality. It is not true that you are stupid because, in this example, you do not know how to goal set. If we continue with that belief, it could be said that everyone who does not know how to goal set is stupid. There is no evidence to support this statement. There is no evidence that goal setting is an innate human ability.

Common Sense

It doesn't make sense to rate yourself in this black-and-white way based on the non-fulfilment of a demand. It doesn't make sense to think that if I don't take action or commit to my goal then everything about me becomes stupid, useless, weak or lazy. It doesn't follow logically to judge yourself in this global way because of a specific failing (i.e. not knowing how to set a goal).

Helpfulness

Holding the belief "I am stupid" is unhelpful and does not support you in achieving your goal. It serves no purpose in pursuit of your longer-term goal. Does this belief help you gain confidence and success? What belief would be more helpful to you? There is no amount of unhelpful thinking that will help you achieve what you want.

Case study: Josie – I must know how to set goals

Josie had always had her goals set by someone other than herself. Be it which degree to take or even what career to pursue, she had been guided by parental influence. Her first job was through a family friend and career steps had been helped by people her family or friends knew. After a successful career in PR, she had become bored by her life. It had been the same for the last eight years and, although successful in her current role, she began to feel that life was passing her by.

Though she found it challenging at first, Josie started looking at ideas about her future, and became clearer about what she might like to do with the next phase of her life. She identified after some fact finding that she wanted to get involved in international development. She had identified some courses but was now struggling to clearly goal set using the SMART principles. Her unhealthy belief about insisting that she should know how to do this next stage was:

I absolutely must know how to do SMART goals. If I couldn't do SMART goals, it would be awful and mean I was incompetent.

This belief led Josie to have thoughts like:

- What's wrong with me?
- Why can't I do this?
- Everyone else seems to know how to do this. I should know how to do this.
- Am I so incompetent? How come I don't know? I must know!
- I'll never be able to change if I can't do this.

Solution

For Josie to get on with this next step and set herself SMART goals, changing her irrational unhealthy belief to one that is more healthy and rational, will enable her to begin setting her goals.

I strongly prefer to know how to set goals but I do not have to know. It is bad but not awful and it does not mean I am incompetent. I am a fallible, worthwhile human being regardless.

In reality it will take time and effort for Josie to start feeling comfortable while setting her goals. It is important for Josie to consistently practise her new healthy belief while experiencing some discomfort while doing so. After a period of time repeating her rational belief, Josie has become adept at setting herself SMART goals and is currently studying her MSc in international development.

Obstacle 2: "It is too difficult and too much effort to goal set" and how to overcome it

Thoughts like "goal setting is difficult or too much effort" are provoked by an unhealthy belief about effort and difficulty. Unhealthy beliefs will be around the general theme of:

Life must be easy, comfortable and effortless.

Some beliefs that may be held around this theme are:

- Goal setting must not be too hard or difficult to do. It's intolerable when it is.
- Goal setting must not be too difficult. I cannot stand it when it is.
- I must find goal setting easy and not too hard. It's intolerable when it is too hard.

There are a large variety of beliefs around this central theme as well as the more specific ones above.

The above demands cannot be fulfilled, and will not allow you to accept that goal setting can be hard and take effort. By holding the unhealthy belief that it must not be so, you will disturb yourself to the level that you will avoid the discomfort of doing it and ultimately will fail at this task. Accepting that goal setting may be difficult and require some effort, that you may not enjoy it all the time either, are not reasons to give up.

 **Reality Check**

There is no evidence that life has to be easy and effortless or comfortable. We all prefer it that way, but reality tells us life is not always so.

There is no universal law that goal setting must be easy and not too difficult. Difficulties can be overcome and not all experiences are easy or effortless. When we hold a demand that they should be easy or effortless, we will attempt to avoid the tasks that provoke feelings of discomfort and effort and not attempt this next step (of goal setting).

 Common Sense

It is perfectly reasonable to wish that life were comfortable and easy and nothing were too difficult. However, it does not follow just because you wish or desire it so that it must be so. You will have learnt as a young child that you couldn't always have what you wanted and you learnt resilience to the discomfort of not having what you want. You can accept the fact that you may want something to be so – in this case that goal setting is easy – but it may not be so.

Helpfulness

The belief that goal setting must be easy and not too difficult is unhelpful. The demand would provoke anxiety at the thought of goal setting and lead you to avoidant behaviour. It would sabotage your goals, as you look for more effortless tasks than goal setting.

Low Frustration Tolerance (LFT)

LFT is a belief that underestimates your ability to cope with an adverse event and is often expressed as: "It is intolerable", "I can't cope", "I can't stand it" or "It is too hard."

✓ Reality Check

It is completely untrue that you cannot tolerate difficulty or effort. You will not explode if you do find goal setting difficult or hard. To believe that you cannot stand goal setting because it is too much effort and is difficult would mean that when you considered goal setting you would break into little pieces – this is clearly not true. You may not like it and may find it frustrating or uncomfortable. But you can tolerate and stand it.

💭 Common Sense

It is true that you may find goal setting difficult and frustrating but believing that the difficulty and frustration is therefore intolerable does not make sense. Something that is frustrating and difficult is not intolerable or unbearable. You do cope with difficult things.

🙂 Helpfulness

There is nothing helpful to you in holding the belief that you cannot tolerate the difficulty of goal setting. It would provoke anxiety when you even began to think about the task of goal setting and you would be more likely to avoid, or distract yourself from, doing the task. You may choose to do something else less difficult and more comfortable. It is helpful to remember that when we choose short-term comfort over short-term discomfort we often experience long-term disappointment.

Case study: Ruben – Goal setting must be easy and not too difficult

Ruben, 24, is in his final year at university studying law. He doesn't know what he wants to do after university. Everyone in his family is asking what he is planning to do next. His father is putting a lot of pressure on him to answer his questions about his plans. Ruben wants to get on with his finals and finds thinking about his future in a constructive way very hard. He has some idea of what he wants to do but is struggling to set goals for himself. He tries to avoid talking about his ideas and wants to put off making these plans. As the year progresses, most of his peers are setting their goals, but he is struggling to do this. Ruben has always had goals set for him by his family and up until now has been happy for others to guide him. He hadn't realised it was so difficult. He is beginning to feel frustrated and anxious.

He believes that:

> **I must find goal setting easy and not too difficult; otherwise, I cannot stand doing it.**

Ruben has been experiencing a really flat mood and doing everything other than his college work or goal setting. He knows that if he is not careful he will miss the opportunity of the "milk round" of major employers and his anxiety is increasing. His unhealthy belief provokes further unhelpful thinking along the lines of:

- I cannot be bothered with anything.
- I do not know what I want.
- Why can't everyone leave me alone?
- I cannot stand the thought of making plans. It all seems too difficult.
- I am too tired. I'll do it tomorrow.

Ruben continues to avoid looking at goal setting and is becoming increasingly anxious, and to party and drink more. He excuses from applying himself to setting his goals because of hangovers and tiredness.

Solution

For Ruben to get on with goal setting, he should challenge the demand that goal setting not be too difficult, and he should tell himself that he can tolerate his feelings even if it isn't easy. To challenge his unhealthy beliefs, he must repeat to himself with some conviction:

I would really prefer that goal setting be easy but it does not have to be. I may find it difficult but I can stand it.

Holding a healthy belief will enable Ruben to get on and goal set as it will provoke less discomfort than his unhealthy belief. Although he may not find the task easy, he will – by holding a healthier, more helpful belief – be able to complete the task. He will be able to overcome any discomfort caused by it being difficult by accepting that it will be difficult. This will enable him to experience a sense of satisfaction, knowing that he has completed the task despite its difficulty. In fact, Ruben, by getting on with his goal setting, discovered it is easier than he thought and he has decided to go on to postgraduate studies.

Obstacle 3: "I no longer desire what I want" and how to overcome it

After spending some time and energy in identifying what it is you want, you find yourself starting to become unsure that what you have identified is really want you want to do. This may trigger feelings of anxiety as you realise you still are uncertain of what you want. Coming to terms with the fact that it may take a few attempts to discover what you wish to commit your time and energy to is normal – many of us experience this. Knowing and accepting this will help you return to Step 1 (Identify what you want) and look again at what you want.

Unhealthy beliefs will be around the general theme of:

I must perform well or outstandingly at all times.

More specific beliefs may be:

- I must know what I want to do in my life.
- I must be able to set clear goals.

and may lead to further derivative beliefs, such as:

- I cannot stand the fact I am not able to set clear goals after all this effort.
- I must know what I want in life. The fact that I do not is awful.
- I am useless: the fact that I do not know what I want proves it.

 **Reality Check**

The demand "I must know what I want to do in my life" is not realistic. Is there a universal law that states that we must know what we want to do? No. If that were the case, everyone would always be in a state of knowing what they wanted at all times. It is obvious this demand is not consistent with reality.

Common Sense

Insist or demand, in this case, "to know what you want", does not make sense. Just because you demand something does not make it happen. It would be preferable if you didn't have doubts or uncertainties, but it doesn't make sense to demand that it must be so.

Helpfulness

Demands are unhelpful. They provoke unhealthy negative emotions, in this case anxiety, which will hinder any progress to achieving your desired outcome. Helpful beliefs, based on preferences rather than absolutist demands, do not provoke anxiety and so you will be able to think clearly and have a greater likelihood of success.

Low Frustration Tolerance (LFT)

LFT is a belief that underestimates your ability to cope with an adverse event and is often expressed as: "It is intolerable", "I can't cope", "I can't stand it" or "It is too hard."

Reality Check

Finding that not knowing what you want after the first two steps is so frustrating that you cannot stand it is not true when you scrutinise the belief and compare it to reality. It simply is not true that you cannot stand it. You may not like it – you may feel frustrated and fed up – but it is something you can stand. Everyone experiences frustration in life, and most often when we do not get our desires met; however, we do not crumple when our desires are not met. In reality, we experience frustration, it passes and we work on finding a solution.

Common Sense

It does not follow that because you do not know what you want to do with your life after the first two steps you cannot stand the feeling of frustration. It makes no sense to believe that "you cannot stand" the fact that you do not know what you want to do, even though you have invested time and energy into the process of trying to discover what it is. It is natural to experience frustration. It does not make sense to believe that you cannot stand it. You can and you will.

Helpfulness

The belief "I cannot stand not knowing after all the effort I have already invested" is unhelpful. It will provoke anxiety, and when we feel anxious we tend to avoid whatever we believe is provoking the anxiety. Holding this LFT belief will stop you proceeding and continuing to consider further what it is you really want to do, and so becomes unhelpful to you.

Awfulising

Awfulising is an unhealthy/irrational belief that when a demand is not fulfilled the badness is viewed as 100% or more bad (i.e. end-of-the-world bad, nothing else is worse in that moment). It is often expressed as: "It is a disaster", "It is awful/terrible/horrible", "It is a catastrophe" or "It is the end of the world."

85

✓ Reality Check

Is it awful that you do not know what you want in life even after putting effort and energy into thinking about it? When you hold a belief that something is awful, you hold as true that it is the very worst thing that could happen. It is more than 100% bad. Is it, in fact, so?

💭 Common Sense

It does not follow that not knowing what you want after the first two steps is so bad that there is nothing worse. At this stage it may be bad not to know what you want, but it isn't the end of the world.

😊 Helpfulness

Is the belief "not knowing" at this stage so awful that there is nothing worse, helpful to you? Well, the answer is no. Of course, there are worse things. Keep in mind that when you hold unhelpful anxiety-provoking beliefs such as these they will not help you achieve your goals.

Self-damning

Self-damning is an unhealthy/irrational and wholly negative judgement of oneself based on the non-fulfilment of a demand. Often expressed as, "I'm worthless", "I'm not good enough", "I'm a failure" or "I'm stupid" and so on.

 **Reality Check**

People are people with differing skills and abilities. This includes you. We are all unique. We all have varying strengths and weaknesses. These do not make the person. You possess both genetic factors, which will influence your abilities, and learnt adaptive responses, according to the experiences in your life. To globally rate yourself negatively and, in this example, as "useless" on the basis of not being able to "know what you want to do having done the first two steps" is unrealistic and simply not true. It is inaccurate, to say the least.

 **Common Sense**

Not only is there no evidence to support the belief you are "useless" but also it makes no sense to hold this belief about yourself. It does not follow that because you cannot do one thing your entire being is now condemned to being "useless". This implies that you are now incapable of doing anything.

 **Helpfulness**

As you consider the above two arguments, ask yourself whether this belief is helpful to you.

Do you think that this self-damning global belief about yourself will help you know what you want to do? Or lead you to begin discovering what it is you may want to do? Do you think this belief will be helpful in getting you to return to Steps 1 and 2 for a second, or maybe even a third, time? Probably not.

Case study: Nancy – I must know what I want

Nancy is 43 years old and perceives herself stuck in her job as a nanny. She comes from a high-achieving family; all her siblings are living their lives seemingly, successfully. Her parents are both successful, dedicated professionals. Nancy is smart and in her life has always played the role of "the joker" in the family, never taking herself or life too seriously – everyone enjoys her company.

She earns barely enough to survive. Her family top up her income in various ways. Nancy has been thinking about making changes to her life and has been thinking about becoming a nursery school teacher. She has gathered information and looked at different courses she would like to go on and has begun to focus on setting some clear goals. Nancy is finding this step of creating clear goals really tough and has started to adopt all kinds of avoidant strategies to interrupt her progress. She blames lack of time, broken computers and other people's problems for not finding the time. She uses humour to deflect attention away from her avoidant behaviour. Nancy is becoming increasingly anxious and uses jokes to avoid the fact that she does not know what she wants to do and to hide this from her family.

Her unhealthy belief is:

I absolutely must know what I want to do now I have come so far. I cannot stand not knowing. I always knew I was a "flake".

She has increasing feelings of doubt and panic each time she thinks of teaching. Every time she thinks about setting out her clear goals and applying herself to the task, she begins to think along the following lines:

- I'm not sure: is it really what I want?
- What if there is something else?
- Why am I not sure? This seemed such a good idea earlier.
- I have never completed anything. I am such a "flake".

Nancy then continues with her avoidant behaviour. Her family are concerned about her but struggle to find a solution other than throwing money "at the problem". This self-defeating behaviour of Nancy's is sabotaging her confidence and abilities to the point she does not believe she can do anything other than be "the joker". When people meet Nancy, they find an attractive, fun-loving outgoing personality with lots of confidence and ease in a social setting. She continues to insist she must know what to do, particularly having told her family about it. In reality, Nancy is becoming reclusive, and increasingly tired from her constant partying (her strategy for dealing with the anxiety provoked by her not knowing what she wants to do with her life).

Solution

For Nancy to get to grips with the problem, accepting that she may not know the answer even after having thought that she did would change her anxious state. She needs to see that she does not become a failure as a person if she goes back to the drawing board.

Her healthy preference belief would be:

> **I really prefer to know what I want to do after investing time in an idea, but I do not have to know. I may not like the fact I haven't discovered what I want to do with my life but I can stand it. I am a fallible human being who is worthwhile even if I do not know what I want to do after the first two steps.**

As you can see in the above example, healthy beliefs are stated as a preference "I really prefer" and the demand is negated "but I do not have to know."

Nancy then begins to change her behaviour and look again at other possibilities, by asking herself questions about what she wants to achieve in her life. When she begins to explore and think again about this, she will trigger her healthy belief. If she does not find something at this time, it is important for her to tolerate the discomfort and build a high frustration tolerance (HFT) of not knowing and repeating the healthy belief that she "will strongly prefer to know but does not have to know" right now. It is important when we are changing our beliefs to practise repeatedly the new healthy belief with conviction. Whenever Nancy thinks she wants to give up as she follows the steps, it is important that at this time she repeats her healthy belief, which takes the pressure off her to find the answer. Over time, while continuing her search, she will enable herself to achieve the outcome she wants.

Obstacle 4: "Goal setting is a step closer to my taking action, which makes me feel anxious" and how to overcome it

This step of goal setting takes you nearer to achieving your longer-term goal. Anxiety can often be provoked by holding an unhealthy belief about the fact that you may have to do something and demanding that you do it well.

It is a demand around the theme of:

I must perform well at all times.

Other beliefs will occur around this theme, some examples are:

- I must do well and achieve the goals I set for myself.
- I must act on the goals I set myself. If I did not, it would be so awful, I could not tolerate it, and it would prove that I was a failure.

 **Reality Check**

When we make demands that we must do certain things, we disturb ourselves, as these types of beliefs provoke feelings of anxiety and often depression, which make achieving the demand more difficult than when we hold a healthy belief. Beliefs that are healthy remain consistent with reality. There is no universal law that states you must carry out the goals you set for yourself. If there were, everyone whoever decided on their goals would then act on them. You can accept that you don't have to do anything even after you have set a goal. It's not a good thing to do, especially if you are passionate about your goal, but who says that you must do anything?

 Common Sense

Holding the belief "I have set my goals so I must act and make them happen" does not make sense. It is natural that you desire to act on them. However, by demanding "they absolutely must happen" does not logically follow. There is a far greater possibility of completing your goals if you take the absolutist demand out of the equation.

😊 Helpfulness

This demand that I must act on my goals is unhelpful. It does not make sense. It has no basis in reality, provokes feelings of anxiety and stops you from taking action. The more you insist that you must take action, the likelier you are to experience anxiety, which in turn will increase your tendency to want to avoid that feeling by carrying out distracting tasks. Most unhelpful.

Awfulising

Awfulising is an unhealthy/irrational belief that when a demand is not fulfilled the badness is viewed as 100% or more bad (i.e. end-of-the-world bad, nothing else is worse in that moment). It is often expressed as: "It is a disaster", "It is awful/terrible/horrible", "It is a catastrophe" or "It is the end of the world."

✓ Reality Check

Remember that how you consider the amount of badness you attribute to not fulfilling your demands can also affect your developing confidence and achieving success. If you view badness in an extreme way, where you judge the circumstances as more than bad – that they are terrible or awful – you will provoke anxious feelings when faced with that set of circumstances. It is not realistic to believe that not acting on your goals would be awful. The fact of the matter is it would not be ideal but it would not mean your world had come to an end. Keep your beliefs consistent with reality.

 Common Sense

There is no sense to the statement or belief "If I did not act on my goals once I have set them it would be awful." The healthy belief that it would not be ideal to not act on your goals once you had set them and yet it would not be the end of the world makes sense and is logical.

Helpfulness

The third challenge we take to our beliefs is that of helpfulness. If a belief is not helpful to you, what purpose does it fulfil? Is it helpful for you to hold a belief that your world is going to come to an end if you do not take action on your set goals? A belief whereby you distort reality and scare yourself by viewing something to be so awful will hardly mobilise you into action.

Low Frustration Tolerance (LFT)

LFT is a belief that underestimates your ability to cope with an adverse event and is often expressed as: "It is intolerable", "I can't cope", "I can't stand it" or "It is too hard."

✓ Reality Check

It is not intolerable that you do not act on goals that you set. You may experience frustration, but that does not mean you cannot continue to complete this step. Believing you cannot tolerate or cope with this is not true. When you hold an LFT belief, you distort your perception of your ability to cope with this.

💭 Common Sense

Does it really make sense to believe that not taking action after you have goal set is intolerable? It does not follow that, because you find it uncomfortable or frustrating, it is intolerable.

☺ Helpfulness

Holding an LFT belief that provokes anxiety does not make sense, does not match reality and has little benefit to you. It will not help you achieve the bigger goals of being confident or achieve the success you wish for. You can tolerate discomfort even though you may not like it, but it does not mean you cannot complete this task, thereby bringing you a step nearer to your goal.

Self-damning

Self-damning is an unhealthy/irrational and wholly negative judgement of oneself based on the non-fulfilment of a demand. Often expressed as, "I'm worthless", "I'm not good enough", "I'm a failure" or "I'm stupid" and so on.

 ## Reality Check

Believing that if you do not take action after you have set your goals proves you are a failure is an unhealthy, self-damning belief. These types of belief rely on globally rating yourself about one single issue. It ignores all other accomplishments, successes and abilities. You have become a failure. This is just not true and is inaccurate. You are a human being who will make mistakes. We are all fallible, after all, and not always achieving what you set out to achieve does not make you a failure as a person. This belief would mean that every time anyone failed at doing anything they would automatically become a "failure" as a human being. This is not true.

 ## Common Sense

It makes no sense to rate yourself in this rigid, self-damning manner. It doesn't make sense to hold the belief that if you don't act on your goal then you are a failure and it's now a proven fact. It does not follow logically to judge yourself in this global way because of a particular set of circumstances.

 ## Helpfulness

If you are still holding the self-damning belief "I am a failure and will prove it if I do not act on my goals" consider whether holding this belief will help you achieve your goals or aid you in being more confident in yourself. You will find it is not helpful in either building your confidence or achieving success in what you want to do.

Case study: Martha – I must demand action after goal setting

Martha is a 28-year-old mother of two, both of whom have been at school for two years. She is looking to develop a business idea she had before motherhood. The father of her children is supportive both emotionally and financially. She has completed gathering all the information around the wine business she wants to set up. She has financially started planning and begun to write a business plan. However, she continues to find other tasks to do. The children, their needs and activities constantly seem to take priority. Her husband has advised her to get some more help in so she can concentrate on getting her goals set and start planning and achieving her goal. Each time she tries to sit down and clearly identify what the next step is, she remembers something else she needs to do and goes and does that instead. She is becoming more and more frustrated and cross with herself and tries to avoid the subject whenever her husband mentions it.

Martha believes that if she specifically sets her goals then she is committed to making them happen. It looks like this:

I absolutely must take action and make my goals happen. If I don't, it would be awful and prove I was a failure.

This belief provokes anxiety whenever Martha considers getting on with clarifying her goals and provokes negative thoughts, such as:

- What happens if I cannot make this happen?
- I've wanted it for so long, maybe it's not really what I want.
- What will I do if I fail?
- What will I do if I get so successful? Who would look after the children?
- I've got to do this.
- I can't give up once I commit.

Martha distracts herself with lots of irrelevant tasks as she demands she will have to act after she has set the goals clearly.

Solution

Martha takes some time and really thinks about what she wants, decides she can set her goals and that it does not mean she has to take any further action. She challenges and changes her rigid anxiety-provoking belief about demanding that if she set her goals she has to then do them and be successful at them.

Martha's new healthy belief looks like this:

I really would prefer to get on with my goals after I have set them but I don't have to. It would not be awful and would not mean I was a failure, whether I took action or not. It is possible that I will not take action, but that would not mean I was a failure.

Martha goes on to goal set, finishes her business plan and decides that she will delay setting up the business until the children are a couple of years older. She goes on to complete the next step of creating a plan so she is ready to take action when the time fits better with family life. By changing her unhealthy belief she is able to complete this step of goal setting and looks forward to starting on the next step.

Exercise

1. Identify the unhealthy beliefs that are sabotaging you setting your SMART goal.
2. Question the unhealthy beliefs by using the following three checks:
    Reality check.
    Common sense.
    Helpfulness.
3. Write the healthy belief down.

4. Identify the unhelpful excuses that maintain your unhealthy beliefs.

5. Identify the unhelpful behaviours that maintain your unhealthy beliefs.

6. List the benefits of achieving this step.

7. Identify the helpful behaviours to achieve this step.

8. Mentally rehearse the healthy belief and take action while feeling uncomfortable.

9. Repeat, repeat and repeat with consistency and force.

10. Take action while feeling uncomfortable.

This third step of goal setting is all about clearly identifying in a very specific way what you are looking to achieve. By doing so you will be able to measure your progress as you work towards your bigger goals that are achievable, realistic and time bound.

By this time you have not only clearly identified what you want, and gathered all of the information you need to know in more detail, but you have also defined a set of SMART goals and are ready to plan how you're going to put them into action.

Tips for Step 3: Set Achievable Goals

- Consistently prefer to do well rather than demanding or insisting that you must.
- Make a SMART goal that is important to you (i.e. choose something that you really want, is significant or interests you).
- Write your goal down using language that states what you want rather than what you do not want.
- Look at your goal regularly (daily is preferable). Make a compelling image of your goal. Visualise that compelling image daily.
- Just before you achieve your goal, remember to plan for your next goal. The natural arousal energy of goal execution will reduce on

completion and to continue to keep motivated and goal-focused it's helpful to have your next goal in mind ready to begin the steps again.

"Man is a goal-seeking animal. His life only has meaning if he is reaching out and striving for his goals."

Aristotle

Step 4

Create a
Plan

"Plans are of little importance, but planning
is essential."
Winston Churchill

The fourth step in the process of goal achievement is planning. A plan is your road map of your current reality to your goal, with a timeframe. Planning is the creation and maintenance of a plan. It can include contingency planning and forecasting of developments, scenarios and how to respond to them. A plan, typically, is a diagram or a list of steps with timing and resources needed to get you to your goal. You think about and organise the different activities to achieve what you want.

You can have an all-singing, all-dancing structured plan or a less formal one. Structured, formal and detailed plans are mainly used in companies, large projects, campaigns and businesses to name a few. Informal plans are simpler and usually used by individuals in the pursuit of their goals.

There are different ways of creating a plan, depending on who is making it, what is available and who will implement it. Individual plans can be as simple as making a list of what's needed and by when. It can be kept in one's mind, in a diary, typed up on the computer or a personal organiser. It doesn't need to be daunting. If, however, you are thinking of starting your own business, you may need to start listing and making diagrams of what's needed but you may also need to write a business plan if you want to apply for a bank loan or to write a marketing plan that includes brochures, advertising, social media, networking and so on.

You already know how to make plans because you plan on a daily basis. You may plan a party, dinner, get-together, trip to the cinema or theatre, birthdays, Christmas and other festivities, New Year etc. You have the necessary basic skills already.

But why plan?

Because it helps:

- Keep your goal in mind as well as showing you the means of getting there.
- Reduce risk.
- Give direction.
- Maintain control.
- Encourage creativity and decision making.

There are many types of plans, for example:

- Business.
- Event.
- Production.
- Life.
- Marketing.
- Financial.
- Contingency.
- Strategic.

The objective of Step 4 is planning and creating a plan, the map to your goal.

Obstacles to Step 4: Create a Plan

It is quite common for people to take time to think and reflect and decide on a goal. If you have decided on your goal but have avoided making a plan then consider some of the obstacles we have highlighted. See whether they resonate with you, and if not think about why you are avoiding planning.

1. Developing a plan is too hard and dull – it's too much effort.
2. The plan must be perfect.
3. I don't know how to write a plan.
4. I'm not sure I want it enough.

Obstacle 1: "Developing a plan is too hard and dull – it's too much effort" and how to overcome it

Avoiding planning because developing a plan is too hard and dull is provoked by holding an unhealthy belief about hard work and boredom. It really doesn't bode well for you if you are serious about your goal. Planning is very important to success and achievement. It enables you to see the road to your goal clearly. It eases decision making: by looking at the steps in your plan, you are reminded of your strategy and objectives. It helps you to maintain focus and to refocus on your goal if you become distracted for some reason.

The unhealthy belief about hard work will take the form of the following general themes:

Life must be easy, comfortable and effortless.

I must be able to perform well or outstandingly all of the time.

The above attitudes will give rise to many offshoot beliefs as well as specific beliefs, such as:

- Planning must not be dull. I can't tolerate dull work.
- Making a plan must be easy. I can't stand it when things are too hard.
- I must not find writing a plan difficult; if I do, it means I'm useless.

We will look at the first two beliefs above and the third we'll use in the case study.

The demands cannot be met if you are someone who finds planning difficult and dull. What we mean by this is that the reality for you may be that it is indeed difficult and dull. You don't have to like it

105

but you can accept it and still do what's needed. Avoidance of this step is provoked by an unhealthy belief about difficulty, frustration, effort and lack of enjoyment. The demand that you must find planning easy or that you must not find it dull is the problem. The low frustration tolerance (LFT) belief is also at the heart of this problem. You are underestimating your ability to tolerate difficulty or a dull task. You really do not have to enjoy creating a plan in order for you to do it. It would be better if you did, but you don't have to.

 ## Reality Check

Insisting that your current experience of planning be different does not alter its reality. You find planning difficult or dull? OK, so be it. There is no universal law that dictates that it has to be different. This style of CBT is not about helping you put a positive spin on what you feel, think or how you personally experience the task of making a plan. It is about helping you understand that by taking the demand out of your thinking, and increasing your frustration tolerance to the tasks and jobs that you don't like, you can develop confidence and increase your chance of success. So we do it by putting the goal-sabotaging beliefs to a reality check.

 ## Common Sense

You do not need to alter your personal reality. You can accept that you find planning dull or difficult. This means that you would have preferred that it were not difficult, because it would have made your life easier. Just because you have preferred your personal reality about planning to have been different doesn't mean that it must be so. This is the common sense argument. In essence: just because you prefer X, it doesn't follow that you must have X. Out of the following two statements, which one makes sense:

1. I would prefer that planning were easy but it doesn't mean it must be.
2. I would prefer planning to be easy and therefore it absolutely must be.

Your demand that planning must be easy or that it mustn't be dull does not logically follow from the fact that you would have preferred it to be nice and easy.

 **Helpfulness**

You may say I don't care if my belief isn't realistic or that it doesn't make sense. You may say that regardless of those two facts you will keep the demand up. It is your life, it is your belief and you have every right not to change anything. But just focus, for a minute, on your overall goal. How is your demand that planning be easy or not dull help you move closer to it? It really is unhelpful. It provokes anxiety and avoidance. If making a plan is an important step for you and you have been avoiding it, then your belief is blocking your success at this moment. If you want to achieve success then it may be helpful for you to change your thinking and behaviour where planning is concerned.

Low Frustration Tolerance (LFT)

LFT is a belief that underestimates your ability to cope with an adverse event and is often expressed as: "It is intolerable", "I can't cope", "I can't stand it" or "It is too hard."

Procrastination is often confused with laziness. If you are procrastinating about making a plan because you are finding it difficult or dull then you probably have a low frustration tolerance (LFT) belief linked to your demand (i.e. planning must be easy and if not I can't stand it). Procrastination is defined as putting off a task that is in your best interest to complete by a specific deadline. At the heart of procrastination is usually, but not always, an LFT belief.

✓ Reality Check

What can we see from doing a reality check? First, if you couldn't stand or tolerate making a plan because it was dull or difficult then you would have exploded and turned into a puff of smoke the moment you sat down to make a plan. This doesn't happen in reality. What you can prove is that you find it difficult and dull. That's it. Tolerate it? You absolutely have been and will. You can also observe that people manage to complete dull tasks or difficult tasks. Difficult and dull jobs do not kill us.

💭 Common Sense

As we said earlier, it is true that you may be someone who finds planning difficult and dull, but if so it doesn't follow that you cannot tolerate it. Believing that planning is intolerable doesn't follow from the fact that you find planning dull or difficult.

😊 Helpfulness

If the reality check and the common sense arguments do not convince you then just think how your LFT about planning is helping you. Does it help to keep believing that you can't stand or tolerate planning because it's dull or difficult? Think about what that way of thinking does and how it affects your emotions, thinking and behaviour and whether it helps you to get the job done. What's more important to you: avoiding the dullness in the short term or moving towards your bigger goal? It's your choice.

Case study: John – Planning must not be too difficult

John is a very successful property developer. He is 46 years old, married and has a 10-year-old son. He works on his own and hires people when he implements any property development plans. He has been feeling down for about a year. It is not serious depression. He is able to function well. He goes to work and socialises with friends and business colleagues. He has been putting off writing a plan for a new property development. He has written so many in the last 13 years that when he sits down to write the new one he feels anxious, then just starts staring into space or surfs the Net. Afterwards, he feels low because he knows that's another day he has wasted. He knows he is avoiding writing the new plan.

He holds the belief:

I absolutely must not find writing this plan difficult. I can't stand the fact that I do. This proves that I'm useless.

As a consequence of this belief, John has been feeling both anxious and down. His mindset is negative and self-damning. Every day he goes to work with determination, then he gets there and has a cup of tea. Then another. He then thinks, "I'll do so and so." In fact, he does everything except write the new plan. He thinks along the following lines:

- I can't believe I'm not doing this. Why aren't I? What's wrong with me?
- I have to just get to it.
- It's so difficult.
- I need to speak to Pete about the new property idea first.
- Maybe I should go for a beer with Pete. It's better face to face.
- I'm so useless, I've wasted another day.
- Tomorrow, I will go to work early and write the plan. Tomorrow.

Unfortunately, John is caught up in this vicious cycle of avoidance, distraction, self-damning and making more demands and promises to double his effort to ensure that he writes the plan the following day.

Solution

John has been writing plans for a long time. It has been part of what was necessary for him do. He did it, he was hungrier and his desire for success was far greater than the discomfort of writing a plan. With that ratio of balance he found writing a plan easier. He is motivated by success but not to the same degree that he used to be. As a consequence he has become more focused on the tasks he finds more challenging instead of on his goal. He will be able to achieve this challenging task by accepting that the reality of his situation is now different. Additionally, he needs to be more compassionate and accept himself unconditionally. John has not become useless, even though he thinks he is (based on his failure to complete a plan). The reality is that writing a plan is just one thing that he is avoiding. In order for him to be a totally useless man he would have to do everything in a useless way: talking, breathing, being a dad and so on. This is clearly not the case.

John will need to understand and believe that this particular failing doesn't mean he must totally damn himself and label himself as useless. Holding onto this belief provokes anxiety and later on depression. He needs to accept himself unconditionally as a fallible man whose hunger for success is somewhat different now. He will need to forcefully recite the following healthy beliefs:

> **I wish I didn't find writing a plan difficult, but it doesn't mean that I absolutely must not. It's frustrating that I do, but I can stand the fact I'm finding it difficult. It doesn't mean I'm useless. I accept myself unconditionally and I accept that I'm finding this task tough.**

This healthy belief is helpful to John and will provoke a state of healthy frustration or concern when he sits down to write his plan. He will be able to focus on writing the plan instead of focusing on how he has to find it. His mind will not be preoccupied with negative thoughts about himself. He will realise that he can get on with it despite the fact it's now tougher for him. The above healthy belief may also trigger John into working on a plan with someone else. He will be open to seek assistance because he will not be judging himself as useless. Accepting himself unconditionally will free him to think of alternative options.

Obstacle 2: "The plan must be perfect" and how to overcome it

This is a common obstacle to drawing up and implementing a plan. We will examine the underlying issues about this obstacle. Why do you think some people demand that their plan be perfect?

There are a number of reasons, but the common ones are:

1. The individual demands that they must do everything to an outstanding level; otherwise, it means they are worthless or a failure.
2. The individual is anxious about negative judgement if they present their plan to others.
3. The individual is anxious about failure.

The above demands are based on the following general themes:

I must perform well or outstandingly at all times.

Others must treat me nicely, considerately or fairly at all times.

Life must be comfortable and hassle-free.

The above general themes can trigger a multitude of specific beliefs, such as:

- I must write the perfect plan. If I don't, it would be awful, unbearable and prove I'm a failure.
- I must be in absolutely the right mood to write the plan. It would be awful and unbearable if I weren't.
- I must be certain that I will do the plan correctly. It would be awful and intolerable if I weren't.

- The plan has to be perfect. If not, I will fail, which mustn't happen. If it did, it would be awful. I couldn't handle that. It would mean I was a total failure.
- I must be able to write a plan all on my own. If I couldn't it would mean I was useless.
- Others must approve of my plan. If they don't, it would be awful, and would prove I'm no good.
- I must be certain that the plan is 100% foolproof. If not, something terrible could happen.

One thing to note is that not all of the derivative beliefs are present with each demand. All or any combination of the three derivative beliefs (awfulising, LFT, self-damning – see "Using CBT") may be present. For example, someone might demand perfection because if things were not to their desired standard (as they absolutely must be) it would be viewed as intolerable (an LFT belief) but not awful (an awfulising belief) or an indication of being a total failure (a self-damning belief).

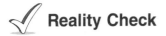 ## Reality Check

Looking at all of the beliefs above, the general ones and the specific ones, they are all inconsistent with reality. There is no universal law which says that you must write the perfect plan, be in the right mood to write it, be certain that it's correct and foolproof, that the plan must not fail and that others must approve of it. That is basically it. If such a universal law existed then all of us would always, and in every situation, and at all times, do things perfectly, be in the right mood to perform a task, be certain and have no doubts, always succeed and everyone who saw what we'd done would approve. It's a nice thought, though, isn't it? No failure, perfect delivery, certainty and everyone approves. However, it is not reality. We fail, we are not always in the right mood, we don't always do things perfectly and we have doubts and uncertainty. Demanding that things must be different won't alter this.

Common Sense

As we said above, it is a nice wish to have. It would be great if we wrote the perfect, foolproof plan. It would be great to be certain that it wouldn't fail. It would be desirable to have others (colleagues, our manager, friends or partner) approve of our plan. It would be preferable to be in the right mood to write the perfect plan too. But just because we want, prefer and desire these things, it doesn't follow that they must happen. It doesn't make sense to insist just because we'd like them to.

Helpfulness

If you have an overall goal that you wish to achieve, then it is important that the way you think and what you do helps you to achieve it. Looking at these demands, it is clear that they will not help you complete your plan. If your plan was an important step – for example you may be writing a business or a marketing plan – the above demands would provoke you to feel anxious, have negative thoughts and/or avoid making a plan. They would impede your success. Letting go of these demands would help you achieve the plan and help you pursue your bigger goal. Overcoming this obstacle by accepting all the possibilities of the different threats and risks would help you overcome your anxiety and feel confident.

Awfulising

Awfulising is an unhealthy/irrational belief that when a demand is not fulfilled the badness is viewed as 100% or more bad (i.e. end-of-the-world bad, nothing else is worse in that moment). It is often expressed as: "It is a disaster", "It is awful/terrible/horrible", "It is a catastrophe" or "It is the end of the world."

 ## Reality Check

If you do not write the perfect plan the world will not come to an end. Worse things exist than failing to write the perfect plan. The same is equally true if others didn't approve of your plan. It is also true that worse things exist than being uncertain about your plan. It would not be awful if your plan failed either. Can you think of what would be worse than all of these things? If you can, then you have just proved that an imperfect plan and all the other possibilities are not the worst things that could happen. We are not saying that you should take an indifferent attitude. We are saying take the horror out of it. It would be bad if all the above possibilities happened but it wouldn't be the worst thing.

 ## Common Sense

It doesn't make sense to awfulise badness. Just because an imperfect plan would be bad it doesn't follow that it'd be awful. The same goes for the other possibilities. It would be bad if your plan failed but not awful. It's not good if you are not in the right mood when you want to write a plan but it's not the end of the world either. Keep the badness but do not awfulise it. This makes sense.

 ## Helpfulness

The helpfulness argument is, essentially, about understanding "what's in it for you if you maintained this belief?" In this case, what's in it for you when you believe that writing an imperfect plan is awful? How does that belief leave you feeling? How does it affect your thoughts? Does it help you to focus on writing the plan? Does it help you to complete the plan? Awfulising an imperfect plan, disapproval from others, uncertainty and failure only provoke anxiety. In a state of anxiety, your mind is preoccupied with scenarios of doom and gloom. You are readily distracted from your goal. Instead of achieving the task of writing a plan, you would be thinking about the "what ifs". It would be helpful if you kept the badness of your concerns realistic. This means remembering that bad things happen and yet the earth still revolves around the sun. What would be the benefit to you of taking the horror out of writing an imperfect plan, having others disapprove of it or failing?

Low Frustration Tolerance (LFT)

LFT is a belief that underestimates your ability to cope with an adverse event and is often expressed as: "It is intolerable", "I can't cope", "I can't stand it" or "It is too hard."

It is particularly present in problems with discomfort, boredom and effort. It can apply to performing certain tasks, experiencing negative emotions, physical symptoms and the effort involved in thinking.

 **Reality Check**

What would happen to you if you produced an imperfect plan or you were not in the right mood to create the perfect plan? Would you collapse in a heap and never recover? Of course not. Believing you cannot tolerate an imperfect plan simply makes no sense. Believing that you cannot tolerate not being certain that the plan is accurate is also absurd. You won't die if and when these things happen. It is true that it would be frustrating. It is true that it would be undesirable and difficult but it is not true that you wouldn't be able to tolerate them. Where is the evidence?

Common Sense

Given what we discussed in the reality check argument, you can see that it doesn't make sense to believe that you cannot tolerate something just because you find it difficult or frustrating. It doesn't make sense to believe that writing an imperfect plan is unbearable just because imperfection, for example, is a source of great difficulty or frustration for you. Which of the two following beliefs makes sense?

- It would be difficult and frustrating for me if I didn't write the perfect plan, but it wouldn't be unbearable.
- It would be difficult and frustrating for me if I didn't write the perfect plan, and therefore it would be unbearable.

Helpfulness

An LFT belief about writing an imperfect plan or being uncertain about it is unhelpful to you. Apart from its not being true or sensible, it really does not promote success or confidence. It stops you from moving forward and sabotages your goals. It creates a mindset that is always focused on "How am I doing?" as opposed to just doing. The LFT belief creates anxiety in the body; often you will try to make yourself comfortable by doing something else instead – the outcome being you don't complete the task. Changing your LFT belief to a high frustration tolerance (HFT) belief would be far more helpful to you.

Self-damning

Self-damning is an unhealthy/irrational and wholly negative judgement of oneself based on the non-fulfilment of a demand. Often expressed as, "I'm worthless", "I'm not good enough", "I'm a failure" or "I'm stupid" and so on.

 **Reality Check**

When you put yourself down – for example for not achieving a perfect plan, for not having approval from others about your plan or for failing – you are operating on the notion that you can, as a human being, be perfect. When you make a demand that you must write the perfect plan, you must not fail or that others must approve of your plan, you are holding the view that you must, absolutely must, achieve this standard. Obviously, this is not the case, but this demanding and self-damning belief does not reflect the true nature of who you are. You are not perfect: no human being is. Therefore, it is not true that you are worthless, useless, stupid or a total failure because you do not write the perfect plan.

Common Sense

The American psychologist Paul Hauck has explained the human self in a very clear yet profound manner. He says the self is "every conceivable thing about you that can be rated". This literally means, all your thoughts, images, feelings, actions and bodily parts are all parts of what makes you you. So if you fail at writing the perfect plan, or if you fail to win approval from others over your plan, how does it make sense to believe that your entire self is therefore a failure? It really doesn't follow, does it?

☺ Helpfulness

Damning yourself in such a final way because of a single failing such as not writing the perfect plan or not having approval from others is unhelpful. It provokes unhealthy negative emotions, like anxiety and depression, as well as negative thoughts and destructive behaviours. As a consequence, damning yourself is directly linked to your lack of success and lack of confidence. It sabotages not only successful planning but also your bigger goal. Accepting yourself unconditionally and accepting that you are fallible affects your success and sense of confidence in yourself in overcoming this particular planning obstacle – another step towards your bigger goal.

Case study: Hannah – I must do it perfectly; otherwise, I am a failure

Hannah describes herself as a perfectionist. She is 32 years old and works for a large charity. She recently became single. She lives on her own. She has many good friends but work is a priority for her. She has been head of communication for the last two years and has to work with many different departments and personalities. Anxiety is a familiar state for Hannah but she gets particularly anxious when she has to create a communication plan. The communication plan is circulated to all the different managers for comments before it finally goes to the CEO for approval. Hannah finds the whole process incredibly challenging and she notices that her IBS symptoms get a lot worse too. Hannah pours over the communication plan in minute detail as she needs to ensure that she doesn't miss anything out. When anyone makes a suggestion or gives feedback, she berates herself for missing something. She is not worried about being negatively judged but is anxious about not doing a perfect job. Other people's comments are a confirmation that she has not done a perfect job.

Hannah has the following unhealthy beliefs:

I must write a faultless communication plan this year. If I don't, it proves that I'm a total failure.

I must make sure that I have thought of everything before I circulate my communication plan; otherwise, I'm a total failure.

As a consequence, Hannah feels anxious and checks her plan over and over again. She brings it up in conversations with friends repeatedly. Her friends keep saying, "Don't worry about it so much. It will be fine. You always do a good job." This doesn't stop her from feeling differently about it. She goes to bed thinking about it, going over it again and again in her mind.

She has the following thoughts:

- I must make sure I've thought of everything.
- I bet I'm going to miss something really obvious.
- Why am I so bad at this?
- Let's just list all the various things again.
- I bet Paul will say, "What do you mean by this?"
- I can't think straight any more. I'm going to get something wrong.

Solution

Hannah needs to accept two things; first, the possibility that she may not write the perfect plan and, second, the uncertainty of not having thought of everything. These two dogmatic demands fuel her anxiety. Hannah also links her worth to these two demands. The only way that she won't view herself as a total failure is if her two demands are met. Her worth is conditional on their fulfilment. Were she to eliminate these two demands, she would become healthily concerned as opposed to anxious. Hannah needs to challenge her two unhealthy beliefs first to help her realise that both of her demands are unrealistic, illogical and unhelpful to her. She also needs to challenge her self-damning belief so that she can see that it, too, is untrue, illogical and unhelpful to her. Hannah needs to accept that she wants to do a perfect job and to be sure that she has thought of everything but that no universal law says that therefore she absolutely must. This is where acceptance comes in. She needs to remember that she is a fallible human being and therefore imperfect. With fallibility comes the possibility of mistakes, failures, missing things out and uncertainty.

Hannah will need to repeat, consistently and forcefully, the following healthy beliefs:

> **I want to write a faultless communication plan this year but it doesn't mean that I absolutely must. There's no universal law which says that I must. If I fail, I'd feel upset but I'd accept I was a fallible person. It doesn't mean I'm a total failure. That's just nonsense.**

> **I would love to be sure that I have thought of everything before I circulate my communication plan but I accept that I may not be absolutely sure. If I was unsure, then I'd accept I'd feel uncomfortable but it wouldn't make me a failure. I'm fallible and I accept that.**

Hannah will also need to stop repeatedly talking about this with her friends. That behaviour only fuels her anxiety. She should recite her healthy beliefs daily and may add other forceful statements, such as:

> **I don't know for certain if I have thought of everything and I don't need to either.**

> **I'll do my best and leave it at that. I accept but don't like imperfection.**

Obstacle 3: "I don't know how to write a plan" and how to overcome it

As we explained earlier, a plan is simply a road map to your goals. It doesn't have to be elaborate. However, some plans, like a business plan or a marketing plan, have a formal structure. It is understandable that you may be delaying this particular step if you don't know what this structure is. There are times when it is reasonable to delay taking action.

They are:

- Physical illness.
- Serious emotional problems, such as severe depression, obsessive compulsive disorder etc.
- Lack of skills.
- Lack of knowledge.
- Unexpected crisis.
- You're reading this book (but not as an excuse to put off taking action).

If you lack the necessary skills or knowledge for creating, developing or writing a plan, you must do something about that. We would suggest that you make a list of all the possible options. For example:

- Self-help books.
- Recruiting the help of friends or colleagues.
- Searching the Internet.
- Going on workshops or courses.
- Seeking free advice (e.g. some banks offer free advice on writing a business plan).
- Seeking professional advice.

Once you have listed the options that you can think of, work out their advantages and disadvantages and choose one. If that option proves unsuitable, go to the next.

The point of the above is to take action to start building on your skills and knowledge because you are focusing on your overall goal. The actions you take should be in the best interest of your long-term goal.

If, however, you are delaying or avoiding taking action to enhance your skills and knowledge then you have hit an obstacle created by holding unhealthy beliefs.

We have found the common unhealthy beliefs about not knowing how to do something are about the following general themes:

I must be able to perform well or outstandingly all of the time.

Others must treat me nicely, considerately or fairly at all times.

Life must be easy, comfortable and effortless.

The above three general themes lead to specific offshoot beliefs, such as:

- I absolutely should know how to write a plan. The fact that I don't proves I'm stupid.
- I must find it easy to learn how to write a plan. If not, I couldn't bear it: it would prove that I am stupid.
- I must not be judged as stupid if I ask for help about writing a plan. If I am then it proves that I'm a failure.

✓ Reality Check

There's nothing to prove that you must write a plan – there is no universal law that states this. Gravity, as mentioned before, is a universal law, where things must fall down. When you drop something it must fall down; it doesn't stay floating up as if it were in space. What we observe in reality on planet earth is just that, what we actually observe. Taking this idea forward, do you observe that sometimes we:

- Don't know how to do something?
- Find things difficult or challenging?
- Get judged negatively by others?

If your answers are yes, then how does believing:

- I absolutely should know how to write a plan.
- I must find it easy to learn how to write a plan.
- I must not be judged as stupid if I ask for help about writing a plan.

alter what can actually happen in reality? It doesn't, because there is no universal law which says these things must or must not happen to you. If you don't know, you don't know. That's the reality in that moment, and demanding that you must know will not alter that fact.

Common Sense

It is completely understandable that you'd want to know how to write a plan; equally, it is understandable that you'd want to find learning easy. Additionally, most people would want others to treat them nicely and not judge them as stupid. These are all perfectly reasonable wishes and wants. Just because you want that it doesn't follow that it must happen. Your demand does not logically follow from your desire. What would be logical is to keep your wants and desires but take the demand out of them. There are very few things that must happen in nature. Knowing something, finding learning easy and not being judged negatively by others are not them and therefore it doesn't make sense to dogmatically insist on them.

 Helpfulness

It does not help to invest in the above demands. You do not get the returns that you want. What you get is anxiety and a tendency to delay or avoid the task at hand, like getting the plan done. These demands are an obstacle to your overall goal. Remember that success is about achieving the tasks you set for yourself. With these smaller tasks out of the way, you begin to feel more confident in your abilities as well as getting closer to your overall goal.

Low Frustration Tolerance (LFT)

LFT is a belief that underestimates your ability to cope with an adverse event and is often expressed as: "It is intolerable", "I can't cope", "I can't stand it" or "It is too hard."

 Reality Check

Believing that you can't bear that it won't be easy to write a plan is absurd. If you couldn't bear it, you'd die the moment you found this particular task difficult. In reality, you'll be alive, breathing and talking despite the challenge.

Common Sense

Learning how to write a plan may be frustrating or difficult for you. Many people find learning new things tough. You may be one of them. Just because you may find it difficult doesn't make it unbearable, though. This is the bit that makes your belief unhealthy. Take this part out of your thinking and you will notice a positive change.

😊 Helpfulness

If you keep your low frustration tolerance (LFT) belief about learning to write a plan, there will be consequences. You will feel an emotional consequence when you attempt to learn about writing a plan. You will have negative thoughts about your ability to learn. You will, more likely than not, delay your learning or avoid it completely. You will get the physical symptoms of anxiety: muscular tension, rapid heart rate or even tension headaches etc. You would be unlikely to successfully complete this step, and this would have an impact on whether you achieved your overall goal in a constructive way. Apart from these consequences, you will not help yourself to feel confident. Confidence builds from experience and healthy thinking.

Self-damning

Self-damning is an unhealthy/irrational and wholly negative judgement of oneself based on the non-fulfilment of a demand. Often expressed as, "I'm worthless", "I'm not good enough", "I'm a failure" or "I'm stupid" and so on.

✓ Reality Check

You are far too complex to give yourself a global rating of "stupid" or "failure" if you do not find learning to write a plan easy or if you don't know how to write a plan. This also applies to being negatively judged by others. No one is perfect. We all have gaps in our knowledge about so many things. We all find some things more difficult than others and we all get judged negatively for various things by others. You do not become a total failure if someone judged you as stupid if your plan wasn't up to their expectations. Your brain would still work, your memories wouldn't fail and your heart wouldn't fail. In reality, very little does fail about you. Therefore, you are not a failure. This argument also applies if you don't know how to write a plan or if you don't find learning about it easy.

Common Sense

The above failings (i.e. not knowing, finding things difficult and getting judged negatively) do not translate into "and therefore you are a total failure or a stupid person". This leap does not make sense at all. This leap into total self-damning from a specific failing is irrational and illogical.

Helpfulness

If you want to remain unconfident then maintaining your self-damning belief is the way to go. You would succeed at being unconfident. But your goal is success and confidence. How does damning yourself for not knowing, not finding learning easy or for being judged negatively help you succeed at completing this step and moving forward? Think about its consequences on:

- Your emotions.
- Your thoughts about yourself and your abilities.
- Your behaviour.
- Your goals.
- Your success and confidence.

What would be helpful to believe instead?

Case study: Gary – Things must be easy; otherwise, I couldn't stand it

Gary is 28, single and wants to study for a business degree. He left school at 16 with a few qualifications and has worked in accounts since. His employer is willing to support his application to study at a local college. His work experience, coupled with a reference from his employer, may be enough. One of the things that Gary needs to do for his interview is submit a work-relevant case study demonstrating his skills in a number of areas, planning being one of them. Gary says he always struggles with learning. It isn't something that comes easily to him. He is particularly anxious about writing a plan to demonstrate his skills. He doesn't know how and he finds books on the subject very challenging. He picks up a book, starts reading and his mind wanders to something else. He then puts it down. He find that he has to read something over and over again, even taking notes, before it sticks. He believes he is stupid.

Gary has the following unhealthy belief:

> **I must find learning about how to write a plan easy. I can't stand the fact that I find it difficult and frustrating. This means that what I've always known about myself is true: I'm stupid.**

This belief provokes negative thoughts, such as:

- This is too hard for me.
- I'll fail anyway. I'm not very bright.
- My brain hurts. I can't stand this.
- Why am I so dumb?
- I can't concentrate.
- Why does it have to take so long for me before the penny drops?

Solution

Gary can accept that learning about planning is challenging for him. He doesn't have to like the fact that he finds it tough. Some people find certain subjects and topics more difficult than others. He can stop demanding things be different and accept the reality. He can also increase his tolerance to learning about planning. He does get it eventually and that happens with repetition and taking notes. He can develop resilience to this by accepting that it's tough but that he is standing it. By remembering that he stands it he will eventually be able to make himself less tense and frustrated. He needs to stop being so harsh with himself and unconditionally accept himself. Yes, he may initially find learning about planning difficult. This in no way makes him a stupid person. He needs to challenge his unhealthy belief by going through the reality check, common sense and helpfulness arguments. This will help him understand that his belief is both irrational and unhelpful.

Gary will forcefully repeat the following healthy version:

> I wish I found learning about how to write a plan easy but I accept that I find it difficult. I can stand the fact I find it difficult. It does not mean I'm stupid. I'm not perfect. There are things I find easy and things that I find difficult. I accept myself regardless.

Gary will need to think about why holding this healthy belief is better than its demanding, unhealthy version. He should then recite his healthy belief, read about planning and make notes until he gets it. He can accept that it may be difficult without telling himself he can't stand the hassle.

Obstacle 4: "I'm not sure I want it enough" and how to overcome it

We have found that some people do not get on with what they need to, not because of anxiety about effort, failure, negative judgement or certainty, but because they are in two minds about whether they really want the goal.

To achieve your goal it does have to be something that you want and is in your best interest. You may want something that is not in your best interest, of course. We've all been guilty of this particular issue at some point or another. For example, we may still want to stay with someone even though it definitely is not in our best interest.

> "I think that having family around helps look out for my best interest. I think that is one of the main reasons I made the transition from west to east. Family around helps keep you reminded of your goals. It also reminds you of where you came from because some people forget and can get lost. It's a great balance and they always look out for what's best."
>
> *Maya Angelou*

In order for us to achieve our goals, we learn to accept risk and take action. This is really about decision making. The decision is either to do or not to do something. In order for us to make this decision we can weigh up the costs and benefits of making a decision and then take action in accordance with our decision.

If you are in two minds about whether to do something, completing a cost–benefit analysis may clarify it for you. Cost–benefit analyses involve weighing up the advantages and disadvantages of two options. The advantages and disadvantages for you as well as the advantages and disadvantages for another significant person/s in your life are identified; both in the short and long term.

The following is a structured approach to thinking about whether you want to go ahead with your goal. It will help you become clearer. If you decide that you want to abandon your goal because you are not that into it, then good. If you come to this conclusion, please go back to Step 1 to review what you want. If not, at least you can now focus on other things. If, however, you decide that you do want to carry on, then write your plan.

The following cost–benefit analysis is obtained with kind permission of Professor Windy Dryden.

Exercise: Cost–benefit analysis

Option 1: (write your first option)

Option 2: (write your second option)

Option 1

Advantages/Benefits

Short Term

FOR YOURSELF	FOR OTHER PEOPLE
1.	1.
2.	2.
3.	3.
4.	4.
5.	5.

Long Term

FOR YOURSELF	FOR OTHER PEOPLE
1.	1.
2.	2.
3.	3.
4.	4.
5.	5.

Disadvantages/Costs

Short Term

FOR YOURSELF	FOR OTHER PEOPLE
1.	1.
2.	2.
3.	3.
4.	4.
5.	5.

Long Term

FOR YOURSELF	FOR OTHER PEOPLE
1.	1.
2.	2.
3.	3.
4.	4.
5.	5.

Option 2

Advantages/Benefits

Short Term

FOR YOURSELF	FOR OTHER PEOPLE
1.	1.
2.	2.
3.	3.
4.	4.
5.	5.

Long Term

FOR YOURSELF	FOR OTHER PEOPLE
1.	1.
2.	2.
3.	3.
4.	4.
5.	5.

Disadvantages/Costs

Short Term

FOR YOURSELF	FOR OTHER PEOPLE
1.	1.
2.	2.
3.	3.
4.	4.
5.	5.

Long Term

FOR YOURSELF	FOR OTHER PEOPLE
1.	1.
2.	2.
3.	3.
4.	4.
5.	5.

Exercise

1. Identify the unhealthy beliefs that are sabotaging you creating a plan.

2. Question the unhealthy beliefs by using the following three checks:

> Reality check.
> Common sense.
> Helpfulness.

3. Write the healthy belief down.

4. Identify the unhelpful excuses that maintain your unhealthy beliefs.

5. Identify the unhelpful behaviours that maintain your unhealthy beliefs.

6. List the benefits of achieving this step.

7. Identify the helpful behaviours to achieve this step.

8. Mentally rehearse the healthy belief and take action while feeling uncomfortable.

9. Repeat, repeat and repeat with consistency and force.

10. Take action while feeling uncomfortable.

This step has been about creating your plan so you can execute your goal and the obstacles that can sometimes stand in the way of making your goals happen.

Tips for Step 4: Create a Plan

- Visualise your overall goal on a daily basis.
- Recall the personal benefits of achieving your goal.
- Challenge your unhealthy beliefs and recite your healthy beliefs and repeat them, consistently and forcefully.
- Complete your plan.
- It doesn't have to be perfect. You don't have to be perfect.

- Accept that effort is necessary.
- Accept that you won't know certain things, but do something about it.
- Accept that you may not have all the skills, but do something about it.
- Accept the possibilities of failure and negative judgement.

"Our goals can only be reached through a vehicle of a plan, in which we must fervently believe, and upon which we must vigorously act. There is no other route to success."

Pablo Picasso

Step 5

Take Action

"A thousand-mile journey begins with the first step."
Laozi

S tep 5 is all about putting your plan into action. After all the previous steps have been completed, you have your plan in place, you know what you want and are ready for this next step. It is time to take specific action to achieve your bigger goal. It's about identifying and breaking it all down into tasks – and then doing it.

At this time you will most likely feel a sense of anticipation and maybe even excitement as you think of making "it" happen. When you set your goals and take the steps identified in this book, you are in a state of constructive motivation, focused on what you want. By now you will have learnt from the previous chapters that demanding or insisting something "must" or "must not" be promotes negative unhealthy emotions of anxiety and maintains a state of coercive motivation, where fear rather than desire is the motivating force.

It is helpful to keep operational goals small. Keeping goals small and incremental gives more opportunities for experiencing rewards and satisfaction, which will increase your confidence. It is important to remember to break operational tasks into smaller ones. They will become more achievable, and by completing them we gain confidence in our abilities and recognise success as we work through the tasks. When we remain confident, we are able to remain task-focused and avoidant behaviours, such as procrastination, are less likely.

There are two important tasks to identify as you go into action:

- The immediate tasks.
- The consistent tasks to ensure your goal is reached.

Immediate Tasks

From your plan you will have identified and written down the critical path to achieving your desired goal. The next task is to clearly identify the first thing to be completed. It could be a phone call, seeing someone or writing something, designing a logo or writing a mission statement. Taking this step can feel exhilarating and satisfying. Immediate tasks are all those things that you can do today and without delay.

Consistent Tasks

These tasks are the ones that support and maintain your progress towards your goal. Consistent tasks are the ones that are done routinely. These are not necessarily the ones that "feel good" to do. Identifying the tasks that will support your goal achievement is vital to success. It is about building good habits.

Examples of general consistent tasks (there will be, of course, many specific goal-related ones too) may be:

- Making regular phone calls.
- Checking emails.
- Action planning for each day.
- Using your plan.
- Visualising your final goal.
- Reading your reminders.
- Data inputting for reliable records.

- Keeping notes.
- Maintaining healthy lifestyle habits, such as regular exercise.

Tolerate Tension and Discomfort

Taking action can feel uncomfortable, especially when we do something new or try something for the very first time. This state of discomfort is normal and does not stop you doing the identified tasks.

Obstacles to Step 5: Take Action

People generally find taking action by far the most challenging step. If you find yourself avoiding or procrastinating about taking action, you may be holding unhealthy beliefs that are sabotaging this step, and in turn your confidence and success. The following are the most common obstacles to achieving this step.

1. I worry that I will fail.
2. The implications of success concern me.
3. I must do the task perfectly.
4. It brings me discomfort.
5. I worry that others will disapprove.

Obstacle 1: "I worry that I will fail" and how to overcome it

This concerns a fear of failure which is provoked by an unhealthy belief about failure. The unhealthy demand for non-failure provokes anxiety, a negative mindset and unhelpful tendencies and behaviours.

Fear of failure is provoked by an unhealthy belief about the following general theme:

I must perform well or outstandingly at all times.

Specific beliefs about this general theme may be:

- I must not do poorly at the task or else I will not achieve my goals and that would be awful.
- I must not fail at the task. If I did, it would be awful. I couldn't bear it and it'd prove I am a failure.

By holding these unhealthy beliefs, you will disturb yourself so much that in all likelihood you will avoid taking action and ultimately fail at this task.

✓ Reality Check

Holding unhealthy beliefs about failure or any combination of the three derivative beliefs will prevent you from accepting that other ways may be possible. There is no universal law that dictates that you must not fail. If this were the case then no one would ever fail at a task. Failure would not exist. You may demand non-failure because failure is viewed as intolerable, awful or an indication of worthlessness. Accepting that you may fail at a task or even that the entire goal will be difficult and uncomfortable are not reasons to stop or give up on attempting the task again or trying to do it differently. Failure is part of life, accept this fact and recognise that it can also serve as an opportunity. If a particular way, approach or idea does not give you the result you wish then discovering a different way to achieve that task can sometimes lead to a better solution. That is what human invention is all about.

Common Sense

When we consider the demand "I must not fail at the task", it makes a statement that there is no alternative to not failing at a task. This is illogical. You know that failure is possible. You may not like failure but the possibility of failure at a task does exist. The demand does not allow for any other option to exist. It makes no sense. We often make demands upon ourselves that make no sense. However, when we reflect a little, we can see how illogical they are. Remember that just because you would strongly prefer not to fail it doesn't follow that you mustn't.

Helpfulness

The demand "I must not fail at the task" is not helpful. It provokes anxiety and a strong tendency to avoid. Your mind will be occupied with thoughts about failing. It will stop you in your tracks. It will not help you to achieve the success you have planned so well.

Awfulising

Awfulising is an unhealthy/irrational belief that when a demand is not fulfilled the badness is viewed as 100% or more bad (i.e. end-of-the-world bad, nothing else is worse in that moment). It is often expressed as: "It is a disaster", "It is awful/terrible/horrible", "It is a catastrophe" or "It is the end of the world."

In this case, failure is viewed as the worst possible thing that could happen to you (i.e. nothing could be worse).

✓ Reality Check

The unhealthy belief "I must not fail at the task; if I did, it would be awful" does not support what life and reality tell us. It is not supported by the evidence around us. Many people, from great names in science to the man in the street, will have experienced failure at tasks and have not found it awful. It may be bad but it is not awful. Holding a belief that has no basis in reality is unhealthy and will disturb you and prevent you from taking action.

Remember you may well think failing is bad – no one likes failing – but it is part of the human experience and the world does not come to an end when we fail.

💭 Common Sense

Does it make any sense to hold the belief that if you fail at a task it will not just be bad it will be awful? It does not necessarily follow that because you find failure bad or extremely bad that it is, therefore, the worst possible thing that could happen to you. Take the horror out of failing. Keep it bad but not the end of the world.

☺ Helpfulness

Is it helpful for you to believe that if you fail at a specific task on your action list that it would be awful. How does this help you? Healthy beliefs support us to achieve what we want and desire. They enable us to remain confident, to carry on even when we do fail at a particular task. Believing that that failure is awful provokes anxiety. It stops us being solution-focused.

Low Frustration Tolerance (LFT)

LFT is a belief that underestimates your ability to cope with an adverse event and is often expressed as: "It is intolerable", "I can't cope", "I can't stand it" or "It is too hard."

In this case, the frustration and difficulty of failure. An LFT about failure means that if you fail you believe that you will disintegrate.

 **Reality Check**

The second derivative belief provoked by the demand "I must not fail at the task; if I did, I couldn't stand it" is a low frustration tolerance (LFT) belief. LFT is experienced when your demand is not met and you believe that you cannot stand it, that it is unbearable and you cannot cope, in this case with the fact that you have failed a task. Is there any evidence to prove this belief in reality? It does not mean because you have failed at a particular task you cannot stand it. Difficult? Uncomfortable? Frustrating? Yes. Intolerable? No.

Common Sense

Accepting that it is frustrating or irritating when you fail at a task makes sense. Believing that you cannot stand it, that you somehow will shatter into tiny pieces does not make sense. It does not follow that because you fail at a task and it is irritating or frustrating that it is unbearable.

 Helpfulness

The belief that you must not fail and that you couldn't stand it if you did is obviously unhelpful as well as not being true or sensible. When you believe that a task is beyond your capability, you will want to avoid it and so will fail at the task. This is most unhelpful.

Self-damning

Self-damning is an unhealthy/irrational and wholly negative judgement of oneself based on the non-fulfilment of a demand. Often expressed as, "I'm worthless", "I'm not good enough", "I'm a failure" or "I'm stupid" and so on.

 Reality Check

You may demand non-failure because failure is viewed as an indication that if you fail you are, as a person, a total failure. This is not true. This belief globally rates you based on one failed task or the failure of the goal. If this were true, it would be true for everyone when they failed to achieve. We would all be in the same boat. If you were to become a total failure, then everything about you would fail, including your heart, ability to think and so on. You would die. This is why self-damning is irrational and untrue.

Common Sense

It doesn't make sense to rate yourself in this rigid, global way to begin with. Specifically to believe that if you fail at a task it proves a global self-damning rating does not make sense. It does not follow logically to judge yourself in this global way because of failing a specific task.

☺ Helpfulness

Believing you are a failure and that it is proved by the fact you failed at one task or at achieving a goal is not helpful. Does this self-damning belief help you find a solution or start another task? No.

Self-acceptance and recognition that we are all fallible, that mistakes (failures) do happen, is not only a more accurate belief it is also more helpful and leads to acceptance of task failures, but accepting our fallibility does not stop us from taking further action.

Case study: Josh – My fear of failure

Josh is 40 and is bored in his current job as a purchasing manager, though quite successful in his career, financially at least. He has a wife and two children, both under five. Life is fairly stressful and he struggles to keep his mood even. It is beginning to have an impact on his relationship with his family. He is experiencing more anxiety and frustration about his life and beginning to think this is all there will be and that he will be stuck in his job forever, supporting his family, paying the bills.

His wife is very understanding and wants him to be happier and recognises his sense of being trapped by circumstances. She is prepared to go back to work to help financially while he retrains, if that is what he wants to do. Josh has identified that he would really like to become a sound engineer and starts gathering information and prepares a clear goal plan. He has identified that the first task on his action list is to book his place on the course he has identified as the best one to get him started. He falters when it comes to putting the plan into action. From being really enthusiastic and talking to friends and work colleagues about his plans, he becomes anxious and begins withdrawing and avoiding conversations with his wife and friends and even begins doing overtime to reduce opportunities for conversations. Josh's unhealthy belief has been triggered by the thought of taking action.

His unhealthy belief is along the following lines:

I must not fail at this. If I did, it would be awful and would prove that I was a complete failure.

This unhealthy demand leads to the previously described avoidant behaviours and negative thoughts such as:

- I'm OK with my current job.
- I don't really have the time to retrain.
- It's not fair on the family.
- I wouldn't be any good at it anyway.
- If I did retrain and failed, it'd prove what I knew already: that I was a failure, so there's no real point anyway.
- I'll stay where I am. It feels more comfortable.

Josh is trying to convince himself that the status quo would be better for him, that life is OK as his fear of failing would only reinforce the fact that he was a failure and this would be confirmed if he tried and failed.

Solution

For Josh to begin taking action, he recognises it is his unhealthy belief about failure that is provoking his anxiety and avoidant behaviours. He takes the time to challenge his unhealthy belief and replaces it with his healthy belief:

I would really prefer not to fail but I don't have to not fail: it wouldn't be the end of the world. Even though it would be bad, it would not prove I was a failure. I am a fallible, worthwhile human being who is capable of making mistakes as well as achieving tasks.

Josh went on to sign onto his sound engineering course and is enjoying his studies. It was not easy to take his first step. It was initially uncomfortable when he went to his classes, but challenging his unhealthy belief each time it was triggered helped him manage his discomfort.

Obstacle 2: "The implications of success concern me" and how to overcome it

This second obstacle is about a fear of success. It is not a fear of success itself but a fear of the implications of success, which can then provoke anxiety, resulting in a negative mindset and unhelpful tendencies and behaviours.

Fear of success can be around all three of the central themes of disturbance:

I must perform well or outstandingly at all times.

Others must treat me nicely, considerately or fairly at all times.

Life must be easy and effortless.

Essentially you are holding the following general belief of "I must not succeed because success would mean [some negative implication]. If that happened, it would be awful, and I wouldn't be able to cope. It would prove I was no good."

Specifically, you may have the following beliefs:

- I must know that I can maintain the momentum if I'm successful, or else I can't stand it.
- Things must not be too hard to maintain if I'm successful, or else it would be unbearable.
- People must not expect more of me if I'm successful, or else it would be awful.
- I must not be more successful than my husband/wife/partner/someone I care for, or else it proves I'm bad.
- I must not be rejected by my friends if I'm successful, or else. It would be awful.
- I must not succeed because I am bad and do not deserve success.

✓ Reality Check

When you hold unhealthy beliefs, it is important to establish whether there is any truth in that belief (i.e. is there any evidence to say this belief is true or consistent with reality?). There is no evidence or any universal law which states that:

- You have to know in advance that you can maintain momentum.
- Things must not be too hard to maintain.
- People must not expect more of you.
- You can't be more successful than someone else.
- Friends must be pleased for you and not reject you.
- You must not succeed.

All of the above possibilities can happen. Demanding that they must not is therefore inconsistent with reality. Accept the possibilities that you may not like.

💭 Common Sense

Does it make sense to believe "I must not succeed because success would mean [some negative implication]"? It does not follow logically that because you would prefer not to experience any of the above negative possibilities that therefore they must not happen.

For example, you might hope that your friends would be happy for you if you succeeded but they don't have to be. They can be as envious as they choose, too: that's down to them.

☺ Helpfulness

The demand "I must not succeed because success would mean [some negative implication]" is totally unhelpful. It provokes anxiety and avoidance. It will sabotage your confidence and success, even though it is completely untrue and illogical. Drop the demands and accept the negative possibilities without giving up on your important goal.

Awfulising

Awfulising is an unhealthy/irrational belief that when a demand is not fulfilled the badness is viewed as 100% or more bad (i.e. end-of-the-world bad, nothing else is worse in that moment). It is often expressed as: "It is a disaster", "It is awful/terrible/horrible", "It is a catastrophe" or "It is the end of the world."

 ## Reality Check

To believe that success could lead to something negative happening – such as producing negative opinions of you by those you love – and that it would be awful is just not true. Naturally, it would be bad if your friends felt envious of your success. Indeed, it would be bad if you couldn't maintain momentum. It would be bad if people ended up expecting more from you. None of these bad things is awful. Worse things exist.

 ## Common Sense

Just because you view these negative possibilities as bad or even very bad it doesn't follow that they are the worst things that could happen to you in that moment. Take the horror out of uncertainty, envious friends, being more successful than your partner.

☺ Helpfulness

Awfulising beliefs are not helpful. Believing that something bad would happen and then that it would be the end of the world if it did is not helpful in the least. Accepting that something negative may happen and that you may find it bad, but not awful, enables you to continue to act towards your goal. Believing it to be awful will not support or help you in what you want to do. Awfulising the above negative possibilities is at the heart of the problem. It provokes avoidance, failure and lack of confidence.

Low Frustration Tolerance (LFT)

LFT is a belief that underestimates your ability to cope with an adverse event and is often expressed as: "It is intolerable", "I can't cope", "I can't stand it" or "It is too hard."

In this case the difficulty of doing better than your partner or the difficulty of maintaining momentum shows an irrational belief about your ability to cope with difficulties.

✓ Reality Check

Is there any evidence to substantiate this belief that you would not be able to cope with a negative outcome of success in the real world? It is true that you would not be overjoyed if after working hard to achieve your goal there was a negative implication from that success. However, in reality, you would be able to cope with it. You would not collapse in a heap when faced with that outcome, however difficult it was.

Common Sense

Accepting that it is hard and difficult when after success some negative issue is apparent makes sense. Believing that you won't be able to cope with it does not. For example, it may be hard to maintain momentum when you are successful, but it doesn't mean you won't be able to tolerate not maintaining momentum.

Helpfulness

It does not help you to believe that you would not be able to cope with a negative implication after attaining success. It does not assist in your goals. Holding a belief that negative implications of success are unbearable would likely prevent you from taking action. A more helpful belief would be to accept the possibility of a negative implication occurring and to estimate your ability to cope realistically.

Self-damning

Self-damning is an unhealthy/irrational and wholly negative judgement of oneself based on the non-fulfilment of a demand. Often expressed as, "I'm worthless", "I'm not good enough", "I'm a failure" or "I'm stupid" and so on.

In this case, for example, you may damn yourself as bad if you became more successful than your partner who has worked very hard and longer than you.

✓ Reality Check

The unhealthy belief "I must not succeed because success would mean [some negative implication]; if that happened, it would prove I was no good" is not true. The global self-damning statement of "I am no good" eliminates all previous experiences or knowledge. It disallows any possibility of "goodness" or ability. The irrationality of this belief is self-evident. You are a complex human being with strengths and weaknesses, dreams, desires, dislikes just like anyone else. Losing momentum or experiencing the envy of friends etc. does not make you no good or worthless.

💭 Common Sense

It doesn't make sense to rate yourself in a global manner based on the fulfilment of a specific condition. It does not follow logically that if you were successful and a negative occurrence took place this would prove you were somehow "no good". Accepting yourself as a fallible human being who is worthwhile regardless of circumstances or conditions being fulfilled makes sense. The unhealthy belief not only defies reality: it makes no sense.

😊 Helpfulness

The belief "I must not be successful because success and its consequential negative implication would prove I am no good" is unhelpful in the extreme. This belief stops you from attempting success and supports the unhealthy belief "I am no good".

This belief will lead you to avoid success and keep you in a state of anxiety and frustration, as you believe success must not happen because of what it would say about you.

Case study: James – I must not succeed

James is the third son in a family of five siblings. He is 42 years old and happily married with two young children. His elder brothers have been very financially successful in life, though are both on their second marriages, and his two younger sisters are married and comfortable financially. James has been offered the position of CEO at the company he has worked for for most of his working life. He is experiencing very high anxiety around this offer and his decision. His wife is very supportive of his promotion. James is not sleeping, cannot concentrate on anything and is becoming quite snappy at work and at home, which is unusual for him.

James is experiencing anxiety provoked by his unhealthy belief about success:

I must not be successful. Success will lead to my family breaking up, just like my brothers, and I couldn't stand that. It will prove completely that I am no good.

James, having watched his brothers' lives, has come to accept his somewhat, comparatively speaking, mediocre lifestyle, realising that financial success comes at a price he is not prepared to pay.

His thoughts keep him awake at night and run along the following lines:

- I wish they'd never offered me the job.
- I am happy as I am. We are happy.
- I know if I take the job everything will fall apart.
- Why can't I just be left alone to get on quietly with my job?
- I just want to sleep. I feel so tired.
- I just want it all to go away. It's overwhelming.
- I don't know what to do.
- How can I make the right decision?
- What is the right decision?

- Work will never be the same either way.
- It's all impossible.

James becomes stressed. His sleep patterns become disturbed and he finally seeks help for his anxiety symptoms. His doctor gives him some sleeping pills and he goes to therapy.

Solution

Identifying his unhealthy belief, James recognises how irrational it is. Highly motivated to get his life back on track, he practises his healthy beliefs:

I hope that my family doesn't break up because of my success, but it doesn't mean this absolutely should not happen. If it did, it would be extremely difficult but I would bear it and I would remain a worthwhile human being who was fallible.

The more rational belief helps James to see his current reality in perspective. He manages to return to normal sleep patterns and discusses his situation with his wife and brothers and takes the promotion. The healthy belief enables him to see that he has options. It enables him to talk to his wife about his concerns instead of bottling up his worries. He has learnt that if his success negatively affected his relationships then he and his wife would figure out a way forward.

Obstacle 3: "I must do the task perfectly" and how to overcome it

This obstacle is about perfectionism and can lead to procrastination and avoiding taking action. It can be a main stumbling block at this stage of building your confidence and success. It is provoked by holding unhealthy beliefs about things not being to your standard and is based around the general theme of:

I must perform well or outstandingly at all times.

The unhealthy belief and the three derivatives may exist, for example, "I must do the task perfectly. If I don't then that would be awful. I could not tolerate it. It would prove I was a failure."

It is important to remember that all or any combination of the three derivative beliefs may be present. You may demand perfection because if things are not to your desired standard you will view that as awful or intolerable. You may demand perfection because imperfection is viewed as an indication of being a total failure.

Examples of other unhealthy beliefs at the heart of this obstacle are:

- All conditions must be right before I can start a task.
- I must be sure that I will be the best or number one when I do something.
- I must be certain that I will be doing things in the right way. I could not tolerate it, otherwise.
- I must achieve excellence easily.
- I must be able to finish the job in one go.
- I absolutely should be able to do the task on my own. Otherwise, it would prove that I was useless.

✓ Reality Check

When you hold unhealthy beliefs, one of the first things we do is to check whether there is any evidence or reality to that belief. There is no evidence that there are any universal laws that state any of the above demands must be met. If they were consistent with reality then all of us would always and in all circumstances work in perfect conditions, be totally certain that we were number one, know for sure that everything that we did was correct, do things correctly, achieve excellence, finish jobs in one go and never need any help from anyone. Of course, we would like to be like this, but alas, it is just not the case.

💭 Common Sense

It is quite natural to want to do tasks well and to do your best. It is achievable and it does make sense. After all, we do not generally start a task hoping to fail: that would not make sense. Why would you bother in the first place if that were the case? To hold the unhealthy demand "I must do the task perfectly" just because we'd like it done perfectly doesn't make sense. Wanting or desiring something is not the same as demanding that it must be so.

☺ Helpfulness

Demanding perfection from yourself when you do a task will tend to lead you to avoid the task. This belief will not help you to attempt the task to find out whether you can do it. It will stop you from taking action and is therefore most unhelpful. This demand will leave you going round in circles: your mind is occupied with thoughts like "it's not good enough, I'm not sure", as opposed to just getting on with the task and then judging your performance. Demands about perfection keep you focused on how badly you are doing even when you are taking action.

Awfulising

Awfulising is an unhealthy/irrational belief that when a demand is not fulfilled the badness is viewed as 100% or more bad (i.e. end-of-the-world bad, nothing else is worse in that moment). It is often expressed as: "It is a disaster", "It is awful/terrible/horrible", "It is a catastrophe" or "It is the end of the world."

In this case, how awful imperfection is.

Reality Check

When you make demands that are in reality unachievable ("I must do the task perfectly"), you may go on to view imperfection as awful, that the end of the world is nigh and that it is more than 100% bad. Does the world come to an end when you do things imperfectly? It is not true that if the task were not completed perfectly it would be awful. The world in general would not stop, nor would your personal world, if you did a task imperfectly. In reality, if you did a task less than perfectly the world would not come to an end, even though you might consider imperfection as bad or even very bad.

Common Sense

Does holding the belief "It would be awful if the task I had completed was not perfect" make any sense? Of course, you don't have to approve of imperfection and it is reasonable to judge it as bad, or even incredibly bad. We are not asking you to be OK with imperfection, just to take the horror out of it. Keep it bad but not awful.

 **Helpfulness**

Is there any benefit to your believing that if something was not executed perfectly by you that the world would come to an end? Does this belief have any helpful aspects as you consider taking action and getting on with your task list?

Viewing any type of imperfection as awful triggers anxiety, a lack of focus and in many cases avoidance of getting on with the job, in this case the immediate and consistent tasks. It will block your bigger goals. Imagine that you wanted to write the copy for a website. If you awfulised imperfection, you would just be writing and rewriting most sentences and paragraphs as opposed to just writing the first draft and then making improvements.

Low Frustration Tolerance (LFT)

LFT is a belief that underestimates your ability to cope with an adverse event and is often expressed as: "It is intolerable", "I can't cope", "I can't stand it" or "It is too hard."

In this case, you would believe that you couldn't tolerate imperfection.

✓ Reality Check

The reality is that if the task were not done perfectly you would feel somewhat frustrated or irritated with yourself and experience some discomfort; however, you would be able to stand it. You would not evaporate or disintegrate. It just is not so. Discomfort, frustration, difficulty about imperfection? Yes. Disintegration? No.

Common Sense

Accepting that it is frustrating or irritating when you do not complete a task (to your mind) perfectly makes sense. Believing that you cannot tolerate the state of imperfection does not make sense.

Helpfulness

Believing that you cannot tolerate a set of circumstances (in this instance a task completed less than perfectly) is unhelpful and will not support you in achieving the task. In all likelihood, it will provoke a feeling or anxiety at the very least which will lead you to underperform or avoid, or take far too long, completing something.

Self-damning

Self-damning is an unhealthy/irrational and wholly negative judgement of oneself based on the non-fulfilment of a demand. Often expressed as, "I'm worthless", "I'm not good enough", "I'm a failure" or "I'm stupid" and so on.

In this case, you may think, "If I don't do this task perfectly, it means I'm stupid and not good enough."

Reality Check

Believing "I must do the task perfectly; if I don't then that would prove I was a failure" is a self-damning belief which can lead to feelings of hopelessness and worthlessness. Globally self-rating yourself as a failure based on whether you do a specific task perfectly is untrue. Think about what would happen if you didn't do something perfectly.

According to the self-damning belief, you would become a total failure. If that were true then what else would you be failing at? Everything, including breathing. This belief is irrational and has no basis in reality.

Common Sense

It does not follow logically to judge yourself in this global way based on how you perform a task. Human beings are complex and have value in their existence. Your value is not assessed on your abilities to do something. It does not mean that because you have failed to complete a task perfectly you are a failure. It means you have done a specific task less than perfectly. Full stop.

Helpfulness

Holding the belief "I am a failure" will continue to stop you achieving your goals, and in this step specifically avoid taking on the tasks that will lead you to the successful completion of your goals. Accepting that you prefer things to be perfect but that they do not have to be and that you are a fallible and worthwhile human being is a more helpful belief to hold and gives you a greater chance of achieving your tasks and longer-term goals. No amount of self-deprecation will help you achieve your immediate or consistent tasks. We don't know of any confident people who believe they are worthless or useless if they don't perform perfectly. If self-damning helped confidence then you would be feeling it.

Case study: Jennifer – I must do it perfectly

Jennifer is 27 and struggling to achieve her goals. She wants to set up an events company. She has worked for many events companies and has been very successful in her career so far. She states she really wants to set up her own business and has planned how to do this. However, she spends a lot of time talking about it but has taken a low-level waitressing job to keep herself busy and preoccupied rather than getting on and taking the first step. She has enough money saved for her venture and a supportive family and boyfriend.

Jennifer admits to feeling anxious but does not really want to face the fact she is avoiding her issues and tends to busy herself with socialising and "networking" without setting her plan into action.

Her unhealthy belief keeping this unhelpful behaviour in place is:

I must get everything done perfectly. If I did not, it would prove I was a failure.

Her unhelpful state of anxiety leads Jennifer to have thoughts such as:

- Why can't I just get it absolutely right?
- I'll look at it next month.
- I'm busy, too busy and I have a commitment to my current boss.
- I have to get everything in order first before I can get started.
- I have so much to sort out before I start.
- I'll start later.

Solution

For Jennifer to stop procrastinating because of her unhealthy belief she needs to change her demand for perfection and global self-damning if she does not manage perfection to a helpful healthy belief that looks like this:

I would really prefer to do all my tasks perfectly but I do not have to. It would not mean I was a failure as a person. I do not judge myself by what I do. I accept myself as a fallible human being who is worthwhile, whatever I do.

Jennifer repeats this healthy belief to herself, especially when she is carrying out her tasks that will lead to her goal of setting up her own successful events business. She will experience a level of discomfort initially until she begins to experience success in achieving the small tasks that will lead to the bigger goals. She forcefully says to herself, "I can do it but I don't have to do it perfectly all of the time."

Obstacle 4: "It brings me discomfort" and how to overcome it

If you demand to feel comfortable at all times, you will become disturbed as soon as you experience discomfort. This obstacle can prevent you from working hard or avoiding any form of discomfort at a physical or psychological level. It can lead to avoidant behaviours that are generally high in comfort or reward. When you hold unhealthy beliefs around comfort, you will avoid any tasks that may provoke any form of discomfort. This demand is in line with the general theme of:

Life must be comfortable and hassle-free.

This leads to unhealthy beliefs that may look like:

- I must feel comfortable at all times.
- Feeling uncomfortable is awful, and intolerable.
- Feeling uncomfortable proves I'm weak.

It is important to remember that all or any combination of the three derivative beliefs may be present. Someone may be subconsciously demanding comfort because discomfort is viewed as intolerable but not awful or an indication of weakness. Another may demand comfort because discomfort is viewed as an indication of weakness but is not intolerable or awful.

Examples of other unhealthy beliefs at the heart of discomfort are:

- I must be able to do the task as quickly as possible or I must achieve results, find solutions instantly or it will be unbearable.
- Life must be hassle-free and effortless for me or it is awful.
- I must be able to achieve tasks without making an effort or else it will be terrible and I can't tolerate it.
- I must be in the right mood when I do something.

- I must feel confident before I do something or I can't bear it.
- I must feel motivated before I can do something.

 Reality Check

When you hold beliefs about comfort, such as "I must feel comfortable at all times", check to see whether they are consistent with reality. If there is no evidence to support a belief, it tells us it may well be unhealthy. Is it a universal law that the above demands must be met? No. If it were true then these demands would always and under all circumstances be met. It is a seemingly obvious answer. When you hold an irrational belief about comfort you will tend to avoid discomfort, which is in fact part of our reality.

Common Sense

It is quite natural when you see other people seemingly going through life with perfect ease that you would want your life to be the same. It would be nice to be in a state of comfort at all times. To demand that it must be so at all times does not makes sense. Just because you demand that something must be so does not and will not make it so. To keep on demanding, however strongly, will not make the rain stop, for example. It does not make sense. It would be great if:

- You were able to do the task as quickly as possible and achieved results and found solutions instantly.
- Life were hassle-free and effortless for you.
- You were able to achieve tasks without making an effort.
- You were always in the right mood when you did something.

- You felt confident before you did something.
- You felt motivated before you did something.

But it doesn't have to be so.

 Helpfulness

The demand "I must feel comfortable at all times", particularly when you are on this step of taking action, is unhelpful. This belief would provoke anxiety and a tendency to avoid anything that felt uncomfortable. It sabotages your success and confidence. You can accept discomfort and build resilience to it. None of the above desires must be met in order for you to take action. You can take action in spite of them.

Awfulising

Awfulising is an unhealthy/irrational belief that when a demand is not fulfilled the badness is viewed as 100% or more bad (i.e. end-of-the-world bad, nothing else is worse in that moment). It is often expressed as: "It is a disaster", "It is awful/terrible/horrible", "It is a catastrophe" or "It is the end of the world."

✓ Reality Check

The belief "I must feel comfortable at all times: feeling uncomfortable is awful" is an example of an awfulising belief. This awfulising belief will provoke feelings of anxiety at thoughts of any task that may feel uncomfortable or challenging. Can you think of something worse than discomfort?

Common Sense

The belief "feeling uncomfortable is awful" does not make sense. Feeling uncomfortable may be bad, but it does not follow that it is awful. It would not be the end of the world if you were uncomfortable and it does not makes sense to think that it would be.

Helpfulness

Holding the belief that being uncomfortable is awful is unhelpful to you. It will lead to the avoidance of discomfort. You will feel like avoiding any experience or task that you did not feel comfortable about. This belief will not help you achieve your tasks or your ultimate goal. It provokes you to find all sorts of creative ways to avoid doing the uncomfortable tasks. What are your creative ways to avoid the discomfort? Do they help you achieve your long-term goals?

Low Frustration Tolerance (LFT)

LFT is a belief that underestimates your ability to cope with an adverse event and is often expressed as: "It is intolerable", "I can't cope", "I can't stand it" or "It is too hard."

Reality Check

In reality we as humans can survive extreme discomfort. Yes, we may not like it always, though some seek discomfort to experience the wonderful endorphin-release feelings that follow severe discomfort! We can and do tolerate uncomfortable experiences, and generally we don't like them. To achieve your goal, you can accept discomfort as being part of the process.

Common Sense

Accepting that it is uncomfortable when you are carrying out a task makes sense. Believing that you cannot tolerate that discomfort does not make sense. It does not follow that because you believe you cannot tolerate discomfort then you will not tolerate discomfort. A task may be difficult, but you can tolerate the discomfort.

Helpfulness

It does not help you to believe that you cannot tolerate discomfort. This LFT belief will not help you focus and complete the difficult tasks that may be ahead of you. Accepting that you may not enjoy the discomfort but believing you can tolerate it without breaking will support you in those more complex tasks, so you can achieve your smaller goals and work towards the bigger goal. Accepting it may be less than fun but bearable is more helpful and will enable you to complete the task. This is how you build resilience and increase your feelings of confidence as well your chance of success. You are not a delicate flower and you can bear it when:

- You are not able to do the task as quickly as possible.
- Life is not hassle-free and effortless for you.
- You are unable to achieve tasks without making an effort.
- You are not always in the right mood when you do something.
- You felt unconfident before you did something.
- You felt unmotivated before you did something.

Self-damning

Self-damning is an unhealthy/irrational and wholly negative judge-ment of oneself based on the non-fulfilment of a demand. Often expressed as, "I'm worthless", "I'm not good enough", "I'm a failure" or "I'm stupid" and so on.

In this case, you may be viewing yourself as weak when you feel uncomfortable.

 Reality Check

The unhealthy, self-damning belief "I must feel comfortable at all times: feeling uncomfortable proves I'm weak" is faulty. There is no evidence that proves you are weak human being because you experience discomfort. We all experience discomfort. It is a human experience. You have strengths and weaknesses. To state "I am weak" excludes all other possibilities. It would literally mean that you would not recover from being weak once you experienced discomfort. Your recall would become weak, you would walk and talk in a weak way and so on. Is this what happens the moment you experience discomfort?

Common Sense

It doesn't make sense to globally rate yourself in this black-and-white way. It is not logical to say that because you are failing at experiencing comfort you are weak. As we have said in previous chapters, this is known as the part/whole error (i.e. believing that on the non-fulfilment of a particular condition the entire self is rated negatively).

Helpfulness

Believing "I am weak because I experience discomfort" is unhelpful. It is not possible that any amount of thinking you are weak and rating yourself in this way will support you in achieving your goals, big or small. To continue to hold this belief or have it in your self-talk serves no useful purpose. Delete it.

Case study: Ravi – I must be comfortable at all times

Ravi is 23. He has finished university and wants to get on with his career directing films. He received much acclaim at university and was showcased as one of the new talents within film both in the UK and abroad. He has a wealthy family who are happy to support his creative ventures.

However, Ravi has difficulty in getting out of bed and getting on with his tasks. While at university, he found everything very easy. Everything he needed to do he enjoyed and was within reach. There were always other students to help out. He was excited to finish university and begin filming and directing his movie. He had plans. His plans, however, did not translate into action.

Without the supportive community of film school, nothing was quite so easy and Ravi struggled to tolerate the discomfort of doing things for himself. Previously, everything had come to him. Ravi was finding he was losing focus and confidence as each day passed. He found himself watching movies rather than making them.

His unhealthy belief that was causing his change in behaviour was:

I must be comfortable and things must be easy. I cannot tolerate feelings of discomfort.

He started having a negative mindset and thinking:

- I can't be bothered.
- I don't feel like it.

- What's the point?
- It's too difficult.
- I'll just stay here.
- It's cold/hot/raining.

Ravi had a real passion for his film making and a great script but he could not get past the discomfort he experienced at thinking of his tasks.

Solution

For Ravi to recognise his issue and challenge his unhealthy belief is not difficult, he is highly motivated to make his movie and get on with his creative career. He is disturbed by his inability to get on and seeks help quite swiftly.

He breaks down his task into small operational goals to reduce his initial levels of discomfort and practises the new healthy belief of:

I really prefer that things are easy and I am comfortable, but I do not have to be. I can tolerate discomfort even though I do not like it. I do not have to give up on what I am doing just because I am uncomfortable.

Ravi begins getting up and working through his action list each day. He ensures the tasks are achievable so he begins to feel a growing confidence in his ability to tolerate discomfort.

Obstacle 5: "I worry that others will disapprove" and how to overcome it

This obstacle that may be stopping you taking action or beginning to identify your immediate first step is based on fear of disapproval. It is provoked by holding unhealthy beliefs about being negatively judged by others, specifically those people who are important to you. These may be family members, friends or work colleagues. The unhealthy demand about disapproval provokes anxiety, a negative mindset and unhelpful tendencies and behaviours.

The general theme of disturbance is based on:

Others must treat me nicely, considerately or fairly at all times.

An example of these unhealthy beliefs and the possible derivatives are:

- I must have the approval from people who are significant to me. If I don't, it would be awful, unbearable and would prove I was worthless.

Other unhealthy beliefs at the heart of the fear of disapproval are:

- I must not be judged negatively by people who are important to me, or else it proves I'm a failure.
- I must have approval from people who are important to me about the way I'm doing something, or else it proves I'm worthless.
- I must make sure that people who are important to me feel OK when I'm doing something, or else it proves I'm bad.

 Reality Check

There is no universal law that dictates that others must like or approve of you or of what you do. If there were, all people would like and approve of each other all of the time and in all circumstances. So if that universal law existed then all friends would remain friends for ever and no one would have a family argument as all people would be living under the same truth. When you examine your unhealthy beliefs and hold them up to the light of reality they rarely appear consistent with that reality.

Common Sense

It does not make sense that you must have approval from anyone just because you strongly desire it. Your demand does not follow logically from your preference. Most of us want approval and positive judgement. That's fair enough. Other people's judgements are their own. You don't have control over them.

Helpfulness

Demanding approval or positive judgement from others provokes anxiety when you face any situation where the possibility of scrutiny exists. It is an unhelpful belief that fills your mind with "What are they thinking, how should I say this?" instead of just saying it. If when you are attempting your tasks you are more focused on what those around you are thinking, you will become anxious and be more likely to fail.

Awfulising

Awfulising is an unhealthy/irrational belief that when a demand is not fulfilled the badness is viewed as 100% or more bad (i.e. end-of-the-world bad, nothing else is worse in that moment). It is often expressed as: "It is a disaster", "It is awful/terrible/horrible", "It is a catastrophe" or "It is the end of the world."

 **Reality Check**

You can prove that worse things exist than disapproval. We know in some surveys people rank presentation anxiety, which is partly due to anxiety about negative judgement, above death. Between death and negative judgement or death of a loved one and negative judgement, which is worse? As you can see, there are much worse things than negative judgement.

 **Common Sense**

If you consider not having approval from those who matter as bad, it does not follow that it is awful. Yes, consider not having approval from those you deem important to you as bad, but stop disturbing yourself by imagining that it is the end of the world. It is not great, but it is not the end of the world.

😊 **Helpfulness**

Beliefs that are helpful to us support our wishes and goals. They support us to achieve what we want. Believing that it is awful when the people who matter to you do not approve is so bad it is awful does not support us; it will tend to provoke anxiety, which leads to avoidant behaviour and yet again stops us from attempting the task or at the very least takes some of our focus away from the task. It is unhelpful, however you look at it.

Low Frustration Tolerance (LFT)

LFT is a belief that underestimates your ability to cope with an adverse event and is often expressed as: "It is intolerable", "I can't cope", "I can't stand it" or "It is too hard."

In this case, negative judgement. It literally means that you would disappear in a puff of smoke if you received negative judgement.

 **Reality Check**

Is there any evidence to substantiate this belief in the real world? You may think that it is unbearable, but in reality this is not true: you can and do stand it . . . people do. It does not mean just because it feels uncomfortable that you cannot stand their disapproval. You may not like it, but there is no truth in the belief that you cannot bear it. The evidence for this is that you are still alive and probably still worrying about negative judgement.

 **Common Sense**

Just because you find negative judgement difficult and tough doesn't mean that you cannot stand it. It doesn't make sense. What makes sense is that you can tolerate negative judgement even though you find it difficult.

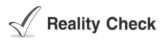 Helpfulness

How does holding the belief that you cannot bear their disapproval help you? It is unhelpful at this stage in your progress where you are so close to achieving your goals to let anxiety-based avoidant behaviours interrupt you in achieving success. Increase your resilience to negative judgement, because you cannot eradicate it as a possibility. If you kept up your LFT belief about it, it would sabotage you taking action and completing your tasks effectively. Your mindset would be more focused on what others thought instead of on your overall goal.

Self-damning

Self-damning is an unhealthy/irrational and wholly negative judgement of oneself based on the non-fulfilment of a demand. Often expressed as, "I'm worthless", "I'm not good enough", "I'm a failure" or "I'm stupid" and so on.

In this case, you may view yourself as worthless or no good if others disapprove of you or anything you did.

✓ Reality Check

The unhealthy belief "I must have the approval from people who are significant to me and if I don't then it proves I am worthless" is untrue. When we globally rate ourselves dependent on certain conditions we rule out reality almost entirely.

Can it be true that because people you care about do not approve of you or what you are doing that you become worthless as a human being? If this were true all people who were not approved of completely by those they cared about would now fit into the category of worthless human beings – ready for the rubbish heap. Obviously, this is not the case. We are human beings and have worth regardless. You are far too complex and unique to dismiss yourself in this way just because you may be judged negatively.

Common Sense

It is true that we fail at winning approval some of the time but just because this happens doesn't mean that we are worthless. Again, this is based on the part/whole error. Failure to win approval means becoming a total failure as a person. How sensible is this belief?

Helpfulness

"I am worthless" is an unhelpful belief and when you connect the fact that you rely on other people's approval to validate yourself you become anxious when you perceive disapproval. You are more likely to seek reassurances to validate yourself. This is unhelpful to you. Learning how to accept yourself as a worthwhile and fallible human being, as we all are, is helpful. Unconditional self-acceptance will support you in your endeavours and help you to be more task-focused and successful than when you hold the unhealthy belief "I am worthless", which will only provoke feelings of anxiety. Self-damning beliefs are a sure way to a lack of confidence.

Case study: Sabia – I must have other people's approval

Sabia is a young mother of a three-year-old son. Her husband is a dentist and fully supports her career. They are happily married. Sabia has just completed her studies in design and has been offered an internship at a friend's design company. After the first few weeks of attending three days a week at her internship she is noticing she has increasing feelings of anxiety and often finds herself being upset and crying on the days after she has been at work.

She finds that she struggles to carry out even the simplest of tasks at work and takes a very long time to complete any task given to her. She knows this internship was what she wanted as she gathered experience before getting full-time work and becoming a designer. This opportunity was the next step in her longer-term plan to become a well-recognised designer in her own right.

She has noticed the other girls in the studio exclude her from conversations and do not invite her to lunch or any social events after work. She has worked hard at trying to build these relationships but senses they resent her presence. She wants desperately to get along with them and for them to like and value her contribution. She finds she is withdrawing more and more at work.

Her unhealthy belief is:

I must have the approval of those I am working with. If I don't, I am useless and unlikeable.

Alongside her physical anxiety symptoms she has many unhelpful negative thoughts:

- I cannot go to work.
- What is wrong with me?
- There must be something wrong with me or they would be nice to me.

179

- I hate feeling like this.
- Why am I so rubbish?
- It is all my fault.
- If only I were better, they would like me.

Sabia wants to change how she is thinking and become more assertive and be able to politely challenge some of the unfriendly behaviours at the office and be able to be more confident at work even if her colleagues do not become her best friends.

Solution

For Sabia to experience more confidence and remain in her internship, changing her belief about other people's approval and accepting herself unconditionally is essential.

Sabia's healthy belief would be:

I have a strong preference for my work colleagues' approval and for us to get along but I do not have to have it. Their opinion of me does not affect the view of myself. I accept myself as a worthwhile and fallible human being regardless.

Each time Sabia recognises she is disturbing herself with her old unhealthy belief or she is in the situation experiencing her anxiety symptoms, it is important that she repeats forcefully to herself in a convincing way her new healthy belief. Apart from this, she will continue going to work and expressing her opinions as and when appropriate.

Sabia is currently enjoying an extension to her internship and is growing in confidence and learning to challenge unacceptable behaviour and to speak up for herself as she once again becomes excited by her future and working towards her longer-term goal.

Exercise

1. Identify the unhealthy beliefs that are sabotaging you taking action.
2. Question the unhealthy beliefs by using the following three checks:
>   Reality check.
>   Common sense.
>   Helpfulness.
3. Write the healthy belief down.
4. Identify the unhelpful excuses that maintain your unhealthy beliefs.
5. Identify the unhelpful behaviours that maintain your unhealthy beliefs.
6. List the benefits of achieving this step.
7. Identify the helpful behaviours to achieve this step.
8. Mentally rehearse the healthy belief and take action while feeling uncomfortable.
9. Repeat, repeat and repeat with consistency and force.
10. Take action while feeling uncomfortable.

So at the end of Step 5, we hope you are beginning to take action on your immediate and consistent tasks. If you have any doubts, read through this step again and examine how you may be preventing yourself from making that first step. The key is to make the tasks small enough to be achievable.

Tips for Step 5: Take Action

- Break down your tasks into the smallest components and do them one at a time.
- If you make a list, only put five tasks on it. When you have completed the list, make a new one.

- Whenever you're working towards a goal, set reminders to keep yourself on track. If you can see it, clearly and often, you'll be less likely to stray off target. This may be in the shape of a Post-it note or a detailed artistic collage or something in between. It can be a written or visual or auditory cue which reminds you where you are going and what you want.
- Begin every day by visualising your goal: see it clearly and then consider what tasks are to be done today.

"Great things are not done by impulse, but by a series of small things brought together."

Vincent van Gogh

Step 6

Keep Focus on the Goal with Feedback

"If you chase two rabbits, both will escape."
Anonymous

The next step is maintaining your plan and commitment by keeping your focus on your goal and having a feedback loop to help you check your progress, find solutions if you are deviating from your plan and make the necessary adjustments or decisions. It may help you to have your plan somewhere where you can see it clearly and, preferably, on a weekly or, if necessary, daily basis. It is not difficult to forget the steps you have planned for. Deadlines are easily missed if you are not on top of your plan. You can do simple things like add a reminder on your mobile phone or in your diary to review your plan and your tasks. You can also create a screen saver of your goal or have a plan that just pops up on your computer whenever you start it up.

Having a focused attitude does not mean having a rigid attitude. In reality, things don't always go according to plan, because you cannot control everything that can go wrong. Epictetus, a Stoic philosopher, wrote about control and said that there are things which are within our control and things which are not. This concept was expanded further by Professor W. B. Irvine, who wrote about:

- Things over which we have complete control.
- Things over which we have no control at all.
- Things over which we have some but not complete control.

It is wise, sensible and logical to accept those things you have no control over and to spend your time and energy on the things you can control or those that you have some control over. It will be to your advantage to accept your fallibility as a human being. You will make mistakes from time to time, you will get ill from time to time, you will experience losses and failures from time to time. You can minimise the likelihood of, but cannot totally control, risk and threats.

You can learn to accept past failures and disappointments, you can learn to accept the possibilities of future failures and disappointments and you can exercise tremendous control about how you choose to react to them. You can choose to respond to past, present and future adversities with a healthy rational attitude or with an unhealthy or irrational attitude. The rational attitude will help you to pursue your goal. The bottom line is that as long as you don't demand that you absolutely should be able to control everything all of the time, you will be undisturbed when striving for your goals.

What we are saying is stay focused on your goal and plan, but review your progress. The review gives you feedback on what the reality of your situation is:

- Are you on target?
- Do you need to adapt what you are doing?
- Are your priorities in the appropriate order?
- Are you on budget?
- Do you need to think of a new plan?
- Do you need to cut your losses?
- Do you have the right resources?
- Have you missed something out?
- Are there any external obstacles that you need to consider your reaction to?

You will benefit from feedback. It will help you to make decisions more confidently, take advantage of opportunities and make improvements.

You receive feedback when you are studying or when you have a performance review at work. It is a significant factor in learning, progressing and developing confidence and success. It would be unwise to either defocus from your goal or to ignore reviewing it to check that you are on target.

Obstacles to Step 6: Keep Focus on the Goal with Feedback

Maintaining focus and adapting to feedback are essential to goal attainment and success. If you find yourself going off focus or ignoring feedback and avoiding the reality that you maybe failing it may be due to the following obstacles:

1. I keep prioritising other things instead, above my long-term goal commitment.
2. I move from one task to another without getting things done properly.
3. I worry that I will fail.

Obstacle 1: "I keep prioritising other things instead, above my long-term goal commitment" and how to overcome it

This particular obstacle can be a real problem whether you are working on your own goals or in partnership or within a team. You may prioritise people, projects, other goals, personal comfort or events like anniversaries or birthdays regularly above your own long-term goals. The emphasis here is on "regularly" prioritising other things. Most of us have other commitments like family, partners, friends, hobbies and other personal interests. The question to be answered is:

Are you regularly prioritising other things above your chosen goal because you hold an unhealthy belief or because it is a choice stemming from a rational and healthy belief?

To put it another way:

Are you operating on a dogmatic demand that says, for example, you absolutely must be available or helpful when called upon?

If you are operating on a rational belief then you need to reflect seriously on:

- Whether you need to change your SMART goals – be honest with yourself and others about whether you can deliver what you agree to.
- Your values, goals and reward expectations.
- How to resolve conflict if you work with others.

You may be a person who cares a lot about other people's suffering and needs and considers it important that you do all you can whenever you are needed. This is a very noble trait but one that can also sabotage goal achievement. We all have different values. You may have some of the following values or similar:

- Altruism.
- Approval.
- Availability.
- Attentiveness.
- Care.
- Charity.
- Compassion.
- Generosity.
- Goodness.
- Helpfulness.
- Kindness.
- Love.
- Responsibility.
- Sacrifice.

There is nothing wrong with having such values and still focusing on achieving your goals. The problem arises if you hold values rigidly and dogmatically such that you awfulise not being immediately available if someone is in pain, have low frustration tolerance (LFT) to the seeing or knowing that someone is in pain or you may damn yourself if you do not make yourself immediately available to help alleviate suffering. Obviously, the above is just one example of prioritising other things above your goals. You may hold other values rigidly that interfere with your ability to stay focused on your long-term commitment and goal.

In order to achieve your goal, it is vital that you make a serious commitment to it and to the means of getting to it. We are not saying become rigid in your focus such that your goal becomes all that you can eat, live and breathe. It is important to maintain balance. The intensity of commitment varies from one person to another but a commitment is still required. Letting go of your goal commitment regularly, for whatever reason, will sabotage your success.

Listening to feedback from others is very important with this obstacle as you may not be conscious of the detrimental effects of your beliefs and behaviour.

The unhealthy belief that would sabotage your ability to focus on your goal will take the form of the following general theme:

I must be able to perform well or outstandingly all of the time.

Life must be comfortable (without suffering).

It will have specific offshoots, such as:

- I must help those who need me straight away. If I didn't, it'd be awful, unbearable and would prove I was a bad person.
- I must be available to those who need me immediately. If not, that would be awful.
- I must do all I can to alleviate suffering. I can't bear to see others suffer. It's awful.
- I must do what feels right in the moment; otherwise, it's unbearable.
- I must do what feels right in the moment; otherwise, it proves I'm bad.

✓ Reality Check

In order to fully appreciate this argument, it is important that you focus your attention on the demand, the must. If there were a universal law that stipulated that you must help straight away, were available to those that needed you immediately, did all you could to alleviate suffering, did what felt right in the moment then what would happen in the world? Everyone would help straightaway, nothing else would matter, everyone would immediately do all they could when there was suffering and everyone would just do what they felt was right in the moment, be it at home, at work, when walking, talking and so on.

Common Sense

It is good to have such positive traits. It is good to strongly want to help, make yourself available to those that need you, do all you can to alleviate suffering but it doesn't follow that you absolutely MUST do that immediately and at whatever cost. It doesn't make sense to believe that you have to immediately. You can tolerate not jumping in straightaway, unless of course there's an emergency. It also doesn't make sense to believe that you must do what feels right in the moment just because you have a strong urge to act on your feeling.

Helpfulness

If you have made a commitment and chosen to achieve a goal then the above dogmatic demands that you impose on yourself will be a real obstacle to achieving your goal as you will regularly defocus from your responsibilities. This will affect deadlines as well as others. It is important to realise that by giving up your demands you will initially feel very uncomfortable but you will be more effective in remaining focused on your goal and therefore more successful at fulfilling your commitments to it.

Awfulising

Awfulising is an unhealthy/irrational belief that when a demand is not fulfilled the badness is viewed as 100% or more bad (i.e. end-of-the-world bad, nothing else is worse in that moment). It is often expressed as: "It is a disaster", "It is awful/terrible/horrible", "It is a catastrophe" or "It is the end of the world."

 Reality Check

The world would not come to an end if you did not make yourself available immediately or help immediately. You can make yourself available later on; everything does not need to stop.

Additionally, suffering is a natural human experience and it sadly happens but it is still not the end of the world. How is this true? The world has not ended because of it.

> "Nothing yes, nothing is awful, horrible or terrible, no matter how bad, inconvenient, and unfair it may actually be."
>
> *Albert Ellis*

Common Sense

If you were someone who cared about others and wanted to make yourself available straightaway if you were needed to help alleviate suffering, it would make sense that you would believe it to be bad or even extremely bad if you chose not to respond immediately. The fact that you viewed it as bad would be entirely personal to you, but it wouldn't make sense to view it as the end of the world. That wouldn't be true, as discussed earlier, nor would it logically follow that just because you viewed something as bad it was, therefore, 100% bad.

Also, suffering is bad. We would rather that people didn't suffer. Awfulising suffering doesn't make sense, however.

😊 Helpfulness

It doesn't help to believe that it is awful if you didn't make yourself available straightaway and when needed, to help alleviate suffering or to do what feels right in the moment. This type of belief will provoke you to drop everything else quickly without thinking, whether it is a real emergency or not. It is unlikely that you would be anxious because you immediately jumped to the rescue. The anxiety would be felt if you didn't intervene immediately. The problem of this type of behaviour is that it affects your long-term goal commitments and others around you. It can provoke confrontation with others who rely on you to remain focused on the agreed goals. The likelihood that you will miss your other deadlines if this is a regular occurrence is high, thus sabotaging your other goals.

Low Frustration Tolerance (LFT)

LFT is a belief that underestimates your ability to cope with an adverse event and is often expressed as: "It is intolerable", "I can't cope", "I can't stand it" or "It is too hard."

In this case, you face the challenge of *not* jumping into a rescue mode at the drop of a hat.

 ## Reality Check

Believing that you could not bear it if you didn't make yourself available straightaway and when needed, to help alleviate suffering or do what felt right in the moment, would not be realistic. You would be able to bear it. You would survive.

 **Common Sense**

You would find it difficult and uncomfortable not to immediately do all of the above. That would be true but just because you would find it challenging doesn't mean that you would not be able to bear it.

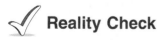 **Helpfulness**

If you want to achieve your overall goal then it is important to reflect on whether your current behaviour, triggered by your unhealthy belief, is helpful. If you respond immediately to others or on a regular basis then you will defocus from your goal or abandon ship too frequently. This will have a detrimental effect not only on your success but perhaps on your professional relationships.

Self-damning

Self-damning is an unhealthy/irrational and wholly negative judgement of oneself based on the non-fulfilment of a demand. Often expressed as, "I'm worthless", "I'm not good enough", "I'm a failure" or "I'm stupid" and so on.

In this case, self-damning happens if you don't respond immediately when others need you or if you don't feel that you did the right thing in the moment.

✓ Reality Check

Your worth is not dependent on anything or on anyone. If you considered what makes you "you" then you would probably conclude that you were made up of your memories, behaviours, thoughts, dreams, likes, dislikes, hopes, successes, failures and every other psychological and biological trait. You are far too complex and unique to dismiss everything about yourself if you didn't respond immediately when needed or if you didn't feel like you did the right thing in the moment. In reality, all of your other traits and qualities would still be there regardless.

Common Sense

To judge yourself in such a harsh and complete way doesn't make sense. It is understandable that you want to always make yourself available when needed or to always feel like you had done the right thing in the moment, but if at times you choose not to do that it doesn't mean you become a totally bad person. This is like saying if you didn't like one piece of fruit in a fruit bowl you'd throw everything in the bin.

Helpfulness

If truth and logic don't convince you, then just think how maintaining a self-damning belief helps you emotionally and in your pursuit of your long-term goal. How does it affect your success and your personal and professional relationships? Accepting yourself unconditionally is helpful. You will be able to decide whether the perceived crisis, for example, is worth dropping everything for straight away or whether you can continue with your goal commitments and respond later on. We don't mean that you need to be heartless and cold, just be balanced about your immediate responses.

Case study: Jane – I must do all I can…

Jane is 55, single and has two daughters in their early and late twenties. She runs a holistic clinic with her business partner. Jane is very much admired by those who meet her. She is kind, warm and has a no-nonsense attitude. Jane tends to leap into action whenever any of her friends, colleagues or family have a problem, particularly if they experience emotional pain or if they need to go to the hospital. She will drop what she is doing at the clinic and go to whoever was in crisis. This means she is often absent from the clinic. She is emotionally exhausted as well but doesn't find her behaviour problematic. Her business partner does, as she feels that Jane should be more focused on her business commitments since she is an equal partner. She thinks Jane needs to find a better balance between being helpful to others and being focused on the clinic. This has triggered many discussions between the two of them

Jane holds the following belief:

I must do all I can to alleviate suffering in others as and when I'm needed. I can't stand to see others in pain. It's awful.

This belief triggers Jane into action straight away when something happens and she will often rush out of the clinic to do what she can. It's an automatic, habitual behaviour.

Solution

Jane will need to reflect on her behaviour and the effect it has on her commitments to the clinic. She will need to decide whether she wants to listen to her business partner's concerns and take them into account and make the appropriate changes to ensure the success of their business, or whether she wants to do something else. Jane realises her behaviour is habitual. She knows that in nine out of 10 cases she could have delayed leaping into action as the crisis was not a matter of life and death. She realises that she is partly responsible for maintaining the needy behaviour in others. She challenges her unhealthy belief using the three arguments of reality check, common sense and helpfulness. She reminds herself of the reasons she chose to enter into business and keeps these reasons at the forefront of her mind too. Jane changes her belief to the following rational version:

> **I'd like to do all I could to alleviate suffering in others as and when I was needed but I don't have to. If I didn't, it would be tough but I could tolerate it. It would be bad but not the end of the world.**

Jane recites her healthy belief daily to ensure it is in her conscious awareness. She also recites this belief when she receives calls from friends who are struggling emotionally. This enables her to decide whether it is a real crisis or something she can attend to after clinic hours. This change is initially tough as she feels very uncomfortable when she delays action but soon finds it easier. She also notices that she isn't getting as emotionally drained as she used to. She manages to keep a healthy balance between being warm and kind to those who need her support and her commitments to her business partnership.

"All the world is full of suffering. It is also full of overcoming."

Helen Keller

Obstacle 2: "I move from one task to another without getting things done properly" and how to overcome it

We have found through our work that another common reason for losing goal focus is that some people will do whatever drops into their lap and in that present moment if they find it more interesting than what they were doing. For example, they may be writing a report but will take a telephone call and start dealing with that instead. They may finish with the telephone call and then go on to respond to someone else's query. They essentially jump from one thing to another without properly completing any of them. As a consequence, things tend to be forgotten easily, leading to additional work and unnecessary pressure and stress.

This obstacle is mainly triggered by the following general belief:

Life has to be comfortable and hassle-free.

The above will have many specific offshoot beliefs, such as:

- I must not be bored when I'm working. I can't stand boredom.
- I must be interested and motivated about what I'm doing. I can't stand it otherwise.

"Procrastination is like a credit card: it's a lot of fun until you get the bill."

Christopher Parker

These beliefs will trigger you to work on anything that is of interest in that moment. You may find yourself switching to another task as soon as you get fed up or bored with it. If this resonates with you then it is important that you develop a high frustration tolerance (HFT) to boredom. You would need to complete the boring task first before moving on to another. You may also need to tell people that you would get back to them and prioritise your day and stick to that but not in a dogmatic and rigid way. That would be unhelpful and would defeat the purpose of the message we are conveying. At the end of the day, you can tick off what has been properly completed.

✓ Reality Check

There is absolutely no universal law that says that you mustn't get bored or that you must be interested and motivated in order to do your tasks. If such a law existed then no one would ever get bored and we'd all be interested and motivated about every task we did. Not what happens in reality, is it? Boredom, lack of interest and motivation are all part of the human experience, a pain in the backside but natural nevertheless.

💭 Common Sense

I don't think we'd find many people who'd say. "I love feeling bored" or "I really like the fact I'm so lacking in interest and motivation." It makes sense that you do not like doing something that bores you but it doesn't follow that you must not do it.

☺ Helpfulness

If you were serious about achieving success and confidence then you would need to accept that getting bored and fed up with certain tasks was completely natural. You don't have to avoid them or distract yourself from them. If you did then you would struggle with achieving your goal and so create future problems. Avoiding boring tasks doesn't make them go away. They still need to be done. You can see that your unhealthy demands sabotage your goals and daily tasks. You may also find that others soon get fed up with you and your avoidant behaviour. They will not pick up the pieces for you forever. It is fair to say that once you have achieved your success you can then afford to delegate those tasks that you'd rather not do but learn to develop resilience and HFT to them first.

Low Frustration Tolerance (LFT)

LFT is a belief that underestimates your ability to cope with an adverse event and is often expressed as: "It is intolerable", "I can't cope", "I can't stand it" or "It is too hard."

In this case, you feel that you can't cope with doing just one thing at a time, because you'll get bored, which you absolutely cannot stand.

 **Reality Check**

It is not true that you can't stand boredom or that you can't stand doing work when you are not interested in it or lack motivation. No one has ever died instantly from doing something dull and boring. You can definitely stand it.

 **Common Sense**

Boredom may be difficult and frustrating, but it is not unbearable. It doesn't make sense to make the frustration of boredom intolerable. It is a mindset, and making this illogical judgement about it has consequences.

☺ Helpfulness

One of the consequences of believing that boredom is intolerable is that it provokes avoidance problems, which ultimately affect whether you will achieve your goals. It also affects your professional relationships. Putting off completing what you find dull may mean that others have to pick up from where you left off. It doesn't promote team spirit. Additionally, if you have LFT to boredom you will find yourself making more mistakes because your mind will not be focused on the task at hand but rather on how to get away from it. This too would create unnecessary future problems and might sabotage your goals and reputation.

Case study: Adam – I must enjoy my work

Adam is 26. He and his brother work in their father's business, an electrical supply shop. He works from Monday to Wednesday and his brother works from Thursday until Saturday. Adam is studying for a business degree and hopes to expand on what his father has done by opening another shop. Adam regularly puts off doing what he considers "mind numbingly boring" and his brother is never amused when he takes over on Thursday. Adam puts off tidying up, responding to emails and sending receipts to online customers. He loves talking to customers and is a good salesman. However, he knows that he is expected to do all the other jobs too, not just those he enjoys. He gets anxious on Wednesdays because he knows he has put off doing all the dull jobs and knows that his brother will be on the phone on Thursday telling him what he thinks of him. His father has also warned him that if he doesn't pull his socks up this time he will be out of a job. He is anxious about losing his job: he realises his father is serious.

Adam holds the following unhealthy belief:

I must enjoy my work. Doing anything boring is unbearable.

This belief provokes avoidance and anxiety when he thinks about sending emails or receipts as well as the following thoughts:

- I hate doing admin. It's dull.
- I must make sure I do all these boring things before I finish today.
- I'll do it tomorrow. I have time.
- I'll tell my brother I was rushed off my feet today.
- My skills are in sales. I don't see why I have to do anything else.

Solution

Adam challenges his unhealthy belief and as a consequence realises it is provoking his anxiety and procrastination, resulting in arguments with his brother and father, jeopardising both his job and long-term goal of opening a second shop. He comes to accept that doing boring tasks is inevitable at this stage in his career development and that it will be to his benefit to increase his tolerance to boredom and do the tasks regardless. His healthy rational belief is:

I'd like to always enjoy my work but I don't have to. It's frustrating when I do boring work, but I can handle that.

As a consequence of reciting his healthy belief and keeping his long-term goal in mind on a daily basis, Adam begins to complete his dull tasks. As he does, he finds that responding to emails from customers is similar to providing them with a good service if they were in the store itself. He later starts to organise his work, doing some of the boring tasks first thing in the morning and without delay and tidying up before he leaves work. He notices that he is arguing with his brother far less, too.

Obstacle 3: "I worry that I will fail" and how to overcome it

Success is very much dependent on the acceptance that failure and disappointments are a part of progress and goal achievement. It is about not seeing failure and imperfection as a catastrophe. It means acceptance that you may make mistakes and wrong decisions. The important thing is to be open and honest to what is happening and to adapt to it. Adapting can also mean choosing when to give up. Highly successful people not only focus on their goals and take actions but also check to see whether they are on target and make changes if appropriate. They do not close their eyes to the reality.

> "It is impossible to live without failing at something, unless you live so cautiously that you might as well not have lived at all, in which case you have failed by default."
>
> *J. K. Rowling*

It is good practice to have a feedback loop about how things are progressing, because it gives you the opportunity to take corrective action if you notice that you are failing. It is important to take responsibility for what is within your control and to accept the things that are out of your control. Sometimes, despite all of your excellent efforts, failure occurs. This may be due to a crisis or economic conditions or some other external reason that affects your goal. All that you can do is to react to it with either healthy beliefs or unhealthy beliefs.

You may be failing at something but instead you choose to bury your head in the sand and pretend it is not happening because you hold unhealthy beliefs about failing. This means that you have cut off feedback.

Anxiety about failing is provoked by holding the following beliefs:

I must be able to perform well or outstandingly all of the time.

Life must be hassle-free.

These beliefs will have their specific offshoots, such as:

- I must not fail. Failing would be awful.
- I must not fail. Failing would prove I was a failure.
- I must not fail. Failing would be unbearable.

These beliefs would trigger anxiety and avoidance of both reality and feedback. You may well be too focused on the hoped-for result and ignoring the reality of what's happening in the present.

 **Reality Check**

Failure and failing are part of the human experience. Given that we are fallible and that not everything is within our control, this implies that we will get things wrong and experience misfortune. You can demand that you must not fail, but unfortunately you will from time to time. Demanding it won't alter this fact. If it were true that we must not fail, we would always enjoy success.

 **Common Sense**

It is disappointing and painful when we are failing at something or when we fail. To be sure, most of us would prefer to be successful and for things to always go well, but just because we'd like it to be like that doesn't mean that it must happen like that. It doesn't makes sense to demand you must not fail just because you'd strongly prefer to succeed.

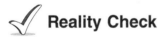 Helpfulness

It doesn't help to maintain a rigid dogmatic demand about failing. It provokes anxiety, avoidance and distraction. The interesting thing about avoidance is that you rob yourself of other options. If you accepted that you might be failing then you would look at what you could do to (a) solve the problem or (b) minimise the risk. Avoiding the reality and dogmatically focusing on the result may create bigger problems. It is vital to know when to throw in the towel too without disturbing yourself.

Awfulising

Awfulising is an unhealthy/irrational belief that when a demand is not fulfilled the badness is viewed as 100% or more bad (i.e. end-of-the-world bad, nothing else is worse in that moment). It is often expressed as: "It is a disaster", "It is awful/terrible/horrible", "It is a catastrophe" or "It is the end of the world."

Reality Check

You can prove the world has not come to an end despite the failings and failures that all humans experience. Some of the failings have been enormous but still we go on and we breathe. There are worse things than failing to achieve an important goal. Can you think what would be worse for you than not achieving your goal?

Common Sense

It is perfectly reasonable to view failing as bad or even 99%, bad but take the horror out of it. Keep it bad, but not awful. This makes sense.

 **Helpfulness**

If you put your money in an investment, you'd want to get a reasonable return. If you realised that the investment was losing you money, would you continue to hold it? Think about beliefs as an investment vehicle. If you are getting the returns then they are healthy but if you are not getting any returns from them they are irrational. Do you think believing that failing is the end of the world is a good investment? Does it help you achieve your goals? Does it help you stay confident and focused in the right way?

Low Frustration Tolerance (LFT)

LFT is a belief that underestimates your ability to cope with an adverse event and is often expressed as: "It is intolerable", "I can't cope", "I can't stand it" or "It is too hard."

In this case, the difficulty of failing is viewed as unbearable.

 **Reality Check**

If it were true that we could not bear failing at something, the human race would not have survived. If it were true that you couldn't bear failing, you would not have survived the failure. It is therefore not true that you cannot stand failing.

 **Common Sense**

It would be true to say that you find failing incredibly difficult, but just because you do doesn't make it unbearable. This doesn't make sense. Clearly you bear it.

Helpfulness

Believing that failing is unbearable would provoke anxiety if you were failing and probably depression if you failed. If you were in a state of anxiety about it then you would be focusing either too rigidly on your goal despite the reality or you would be focused on the problem as opposed to solving the problem. Neither is helpful to you.

Self-damning

Self-damning is an unhealthy/irrational and wholly negative judgement of oneself based on the non-fulfilment of a demand. Often expressed as, "I'm worthless", "I'm not good enough", "I'm a failure" or "I'm stupid" and so on.

In this case, you might label yourself as a failure or worthless if you were failing at your goal.

Reality Check

It is clearly not true that if you fail at something you become a total failure. If that were true, your brain would and everything else about you would fail too. You would die instantly the moment you realised that you were failing. If you are reading this then you have proved you are not a total failure.

Common Sense

Failing at something is tangible. You can judge it, quantify it and qualify it. It's distinct. Just because you may fail at something does not mean that you become a total failure. It just means you failed at X at that time in your life. That's it.

☺ Helpfulness

To believe that you are a total failure because you may be failing in achieving your goal is untrue and lacks common sense, but if you don't change your attitude about yourself then you may well find yourself experiencing emotional, mental, behavioural and physical problems. In such a state you are far less likely to either minimise the negative results or think of constructive solutions. Either way, you will fail and remain disturbed for too long. It's in your interest to be more compassionate about yourself and accept yourself unconditionally as a fallible human being.

Case study: Robert – I must not fail

Robert is a 45-year-old self-employed business man who is in a long-term relationship. He started his import and export agency four years ago. He knew at that time that he was taking a risk but he was excited about being his own boss after working in a multinational company for 10 years. Robert did everything by the book. He set himself a SMART goal, made a detailed plan and implemented it. He works hard on a daily basis. Sadly, he is just keeping his head above water. His partner is very happy to be the major breadwinner so that is not a problem.

Robert avoids questions about how his business is doing. He makes vague statements like "It's fine", "It could be better" and so on. He is anxious about what is happening but resists facing the reality of his venture. He just carries on.

Robert is holding the following belief:

I have to make sure this works. It would be awful if I allowed it to fail.

Robert does not accept that he is not totally in control and believes that he must not allow it to fail. Despite the reality of economic conditions, he is refusing to face it.

His belief provokes the following thoughts:

- It has to work out.
- I'll just keep doing what I'm doing. Something will change.
- It would be awful if this didn't work out.
- What will I do?
- What will I say?
- I've spent four years on this. I can't give up.

This belief and the above thoughts provoke anxiety and Robert starts to suffer from insomnia, ruminating about what else he can do.

Solution

In order for Robert to become healthy and rational about his work, he will need to change his belief and accept the reality of what is happening at the moment. His new belief will be:

I really hope this works out but it absolutely doesn't have to. If it fails, that would be incredibly bad but it wouldn't be the worst thing that could happen to me.

By facing the reality of what is happening and accepting the possibility that his business is failing Robert becomes more solution-focused and pragmatic. He forcefully repeats his healthy belief and makes a contingency plan. He realises that by facing his current reality he can choose to cut some costs and work from home instead. He also decides to give it one more year and then review. He thinks of the following options when the year is up:

- Get a full-time job and fold his business.
- Get a part-time job and continue with his business on a part-time basis.
- Start a new business venture and learn from this one.

He is now able to feel more confident as he knows the world won't come to end if his business folds and that he has options.

Exercise – maintaining focus

1. Identify your unhealthy beliefs that are sabotaging you maintaining focus.
2. Question the unhealthy beliefs by using the following three checks:

   Reality check.

   Common sense.

   Helpfulness.
3. Write the healthy belief down.
4. Identify the unhelpful excuses that maintain your unhealthy beliefs.
5. Identify the unhelpful behaviours that maintain your unhealthy beliefs.
6. List the benefits of achieving this step.
7. Identify the helpful behaviours to achieve this step.
8. Mentally rehearse the healthy belief and take action while feeling uncomfortable.
9. Repeat, repeat and repeat with consistency and force.
10. Take action while feeling uncomfortable.

This step has been about maintaining focus on your goals while adapting to feedback and looking at the obstacles that distract us from maintaining focus on our goals, and using feedback to review and adapt if the need arises. Three common obstacles were discussed and overcome by looking at the unhealthy beliefs that create them. The obstacles were giving yourself permission to regularly prioritise other things above your long-term goal commitment, moving from one task to another without getting things done properly and the fear of failing.

Tips for Step 6: Keep Focus on the Goal with Feedback

- Visualise and focus on your goal on a daily basis.
- Create a feedback loop where you regularly check your progress. Be open and honest.
- Adapt and don't be rigid in your focus.
- Accept failure and that failing can happen. Do not disturb yourself about them.
- If you fail, learn from it without beating yourself up about it. Get up and do it again if you want.
- Have a contingency plan.
- Learn when to give up.

Goal Achieved – Now What?

Having completed all the steps, you should now be taking immediate and consistent action and moving towards greater confidence and success. The likelihood of achieving your bigger goals is in your favour, taking external factors into account.

So what is next after you achieve your goal? Take some time to review what you have achieved, reflect on it and how you can learn from that experience and apply any learning to your next goal. Then, well it's up to you! You can continue maintaining what you are doing or you can set new goals for yourself. Bigger ones, perhaps? To grow and develop it is important that we stretch our comfort zone. This means putting ourselves in new challenging situations. Remember it is helpful to start setting new goals just before your achieve the current one as this keeps your energy and momentum up. The mind provides just enough energy for us to accomplish a goal.

It is quite natural that when you have been busy and focused on your tasks that when you have reached your goal there is nothing left to do. This leaves a space. If you choose not to start this process again, you may find yourself feeling a level of discomfort, as you adjust to less activity. This is transient and you do not have to disturb yourself about it. You can just sit with this discomfort, choosing to reflect or not to reflect on what to do next.

You may choose to relax and unwind but as in marathon running it is never advisable to just stop training all together after completing a marathon. You can continue on a reduced programme as you manage the reduction of required energy. The same applies to all goals and goal attainment.

If we do not plan for the post-goal attainment period we may find the lack of focus and goals uncomfortable and may trigger unhealthy beliefs about discomfort or purpose in life. You can work through any unhealthy beliefs by applying the three arguments and formulating the healthy beliefs and strengthening them by thinking and acting accordingly. We are, sadly, never immune to creating unhealthy beliefs. It is in our nature. Accept it but learn to challenge it as and when it happens. To maintain confidence and a sense of success, the steps in this book should, preferably, become a lifetime practice.

Case study: Jo and Sophie – What next?

Jo and Sophie have worked together in their own business for the last 15 years. Two years ago, they sold it to a large international company. They had a two-year work-out clause in the contract. They had achieved their goal in spectacular style. Both now had the freedom financially to pretty much do what they wanted. What did they want? Both Jo and Sophie had been working so hard and in such a focused way that as their contract was coming to a close they both experienced symptoms of anxiety as the day loomed when they would have no office to go to, no deadline to meet. Both had families and homes they had managed while working. Just being at home was not appealing.

They both experienced the physical sensations of anxiety and their thoughts were constantly awfulising the possibility of not knowing what they wanted. It took some time for each of them to consider what to do next. And not knowing what they wanted prompted unhealthy beliefs:

> **I must know what I want to do next; otherwise, it would be awful. I couldn't bear it.**
>
> *Solution*
>
> Once they recognised it was quite normal to question what to do next and to receive the answer "nothing", they stopped holding this unhealthy belief. Jo and Sophie changed their unhealthy belief to the healthy one of:
>
> **I prefer to know what I want to do in the future but I do not have to. It is not the end of the world that I do not know what I want to do in the future.**
>
> Their future plans formulated over time and continue to do so. Once the unhealthy belief changed, the anxiety provoked by it reduced and they were able to plan without demanding that they had to know immediately or exactly.

Once you have realised your goal, it is useful to reflect on what you have achieved, how you achieved it and on what you would do differently next time.

With the experience of having achieved this goal, review the rest of your goal plans:

- If you achieved the goal too easily, make your next goal bigger or more challenging.
- If the goal took a dispiriting length of time to achieve, make the next goal a little easier.
- If you learnt something that would lead you to change other goals, do so.
- If you noticed a deficit in your skills despite achieving the goal, decide whether to set goals to fix this.

Goal setting is a life skill, and one that you use throughout your life. We hope you have found this book helpful in achieving your goals, gaining more confidence and achieving the success you desired.

We are off to set our next goal now – what about you?

> "Far better it is to dare mighty things, to win glorious triumphs even though checkered by failure, than to rank with those poor spirits who neither enjoy nor suffer much because they live in the gray twilight that knows neither victory nor defeat."
>
> *Theodore Roosevelt*

Some Final Tips to Remember . . . for Whatever Step You Are on

- Do not label yourself.
- Take immediate action.
- Accept tension and discomfort as natural.
- Accept uncertainty and risk.
- Develop a high frustration tolerance philosophy.
- Develop an anti-awfulising philosophy.
- Accept yourself. You are a worthwhile but fallible human being.
- Develop enlightened self-interest.
- Give up your creative excuses and pseudo-work.
- Do one task at a time – do not jump from one task to another.
- Tolerate an imperfect environment.
- Manage your excesses – alcohol, overeating, recreational drugs.
- Keep an eye on your goal.
- Make your environment work for you.
- Look for solutions when facing problems and learn from your mistakes.
- Allocate extra time to complete a task as things can go wrong.
- Be assertive.

- Reward yourself when you have completed a task, e.g. tea break, ten-minute walk.
- Break a task into chunks.
- Start with committing yourself to spending five minutes on the task and go on from there.
- Do the unpleasant task first and immediately.
- Imagine yourself doing the task.
- Procrastination is your cue to force yourself to do the task.

About the Authors

Avy Joseph

Avy is the Principal, Director and Co-founder of the College of Cognitive Behavioural Therapies (CCBT) and City Minds. He is a registered and accredited therapist with the British Association for Behavioural and Cognitive Psychotherapies (BABCP) and a board member of the Association of Rational Emotive Behaviour Therapists (AREBT).

Avy began working as a counsellor and therapist over twenty years ago, developing and running workshops on Relationship Problems, Phobias, Panic Disorders as well as Goal Achievement. It was when lecturing both nationally and internationally that his interest in evidence-based cognitive behaviour therapy (CBT) grew. He went on to gain a master's degree in rational-emotive behaviour therapy from Goldsmiths College (one of the main schools of cognitive and behavioural therapy). He has recently published *Visual CBT* with Maggie Chapman, Co-Founder of the College. Other published works include *Cognitive Behavioural Therapy: Your route out of perfectionism, self-sabotage and other everyday habits*.

Maggie Chapman

Maggie is a Director and Co-founder of the College of Cognitive Behavioural Therapies (CCBT) and City Minds. She is an experienced therapist who, with over twenty years' experience, has developed an integrative approach to her work, employing CBT and brief, solution-focused strategies.

Following an initial career in business, Maggie gained a degree in psychology and retrained as a trauma and bereavement counsellor before going on to lecture for many years both nationally and internationally, developing many courses, seminars and workshops, which have culminated in the development of specialised courses at the College. She has private practices in central and south-west London. She has recently published *Visual CBT* with Avy Joseph.

Acknowledgements

We would like to thank all those who have supported, guided and helped us, both over the years and in the development of this book, and in particular:

Windy Dryden, for his support and guidance.

Our clients, who have informed our work.

Our colleagues and students at CCBT.

Holly and Jenny at Capstone for all their wonderful support and input – they have been amazing.

Maggie, to her sons, Remi and Massih.

Avy, to his mother, Lily Joseph.

Index